CULTURE SMART!

SINGAPORE

Angela Milligan

Graphic Arts Center Publishing®

First published in Great Britain 2004
by Kuperard, an imprint of Bravo Ltd.

Series Editor Geoffrey Chesler
Design DW Design

Simultaneously published in the U.S.A. and Canada
by Graphic Arts Center Publishing Company
P. O. Box 10306, Portland, OR 97296-0306

Library of Congress Cataloging-in-Publication Data

Milligan, Angela.
Singapore : a quick guide to customs and etiquette / Angela Milligan.

    p. cm. – (Culture smart!)
Includes bibliographical references and index.
ISBN 1-55868-789-0 (softbound)
1. Singapore–Social life and customs. 2. Etiquette–Singapore.
3. National characteristics, Singapore. I. Title. II. Series.
DS609.9.M55 2004
959.57–dc22

                    2004004446

Printed in Hong Kong

Cover image: Merlion statue, Singapore.
Travel Ink/Geoffrey Clive

About the Author

ANGELA MILLIGAN specializes in preparing individuals and families from Europe and North America for expatriate life, an important aspect of which is cultural awareness training. She has lived and worked in many parts of East Asia, as well as in Australia, Belgium, and the Argentine, and has briefed several major international companies on Singapore. Her publications include *How to Survive in Style*, a practical reference guide for newly arrived expatriates to Britain, and the *Simple Guide to Australia*. Angela is a graduate in history from the University of East Anglia and a Fellow of the Royal Society of Arts.

Other Books in the Series

- Culture Smart! Australia
- Culture Smart! Britain
- Culture Smart! China
- Culture Smart! Finland
- Culture Smart! France
- Culture Smart! Germany
- Culture Smart! Greece
- Culture Smart! Hong Kong
- Culture Smart! India
- Culture Smart! Ireland
- Culture Smart! Italy
- Culture Smart! Japan

- Culture Smart! Korea
- Culture Smart! Mexico
- Culture Smart! Netherlands
- Culture Smart! Philippines
- Culture Smart! Poland
- Culture Smart! Russia
- Culture Smart! Spain
- Culture Smart! Sweden
- Culture Smart! Switzerland
- Culture Smart! Thailand
- Culture Smart! USA

Other titles are in preparation. For more information, contact: info@kuperard.co.uk

The publishers would like to thank **CultureShock!**Consulting for its help in researching and developing the concept for this series.

CultureShock!Consulting

We are all likely at some time to be dealing with other cultures—foreign visitors at home, e-mails from abroad, overseas sales agents, multicultural teams within our organization, or a new foreign management structure.

CultureShock!Consulting creates tailor-made seminars and consultancy programs to meet all types of corporate, public sector, and individual intercultural needs. It provides pre- and post-assignment programs, as well as ongoing "in-the-field" counseling worldwide.

For details, see www.cultureshockconsulting.com

contents

contents

Map of Singapore

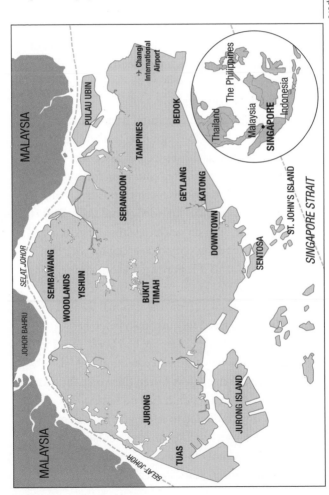

introduction

The small island state of Singapore is unique in the region. Not only is it a very young country—independence came in 1965—but it is a land of immigrants, in which people from three distinct backgrounds, Chinese, Malay, and Indian, live side by side in harmony.

Singapore's multicultural harmony is no accident. From the beginning, realizing that its people were its most precious asset, the government made free education for all a national priority, with schools teaching positive attitudes as well as essential knowledge and skills. This is an energetic, "can do" society, whose citizens are often worried about not keeping up with the Joneses, or, as it is portrayed in Singapore, "*kiasu*," from the Hokkien word meaning "to miss out."

On August 9, 1965, the national leader Lee Kuan Yew faced the unknown when he announced that Singapore had been forced to leave the newly formed Federation of Malaysia. Many commentators feared the worst, for this newly created republic had no natural resources, was tiny compared to its neighbors, and only had its deep water harbor, its commercial skills, and its close proximity to the rest of Asia to rely on. Within fifteen years, however, Singapore had transformed itself into an economic powerhouse and become a byword for technical excellence.

Yet despite its Western veneer, the visitor is quickly reminded that the "Lion City" is most definitely Asian. Although many of the traditional cultural values of the communities living there have been challenged by the demands of the modern Singaporean state, their underlying philosophies remain intact. It is therefore difficult to talk about a typical Singaporean, for this would depend on whether one were referring to someone of Chinese, Malay, or Indian descent. By and large, however, this is a very goal-oriented, meritocratic society. It is also fair to say that the three ethnic groups share certain Asian values— belief in ordered relationships, obligation, respect for traditions, polite behavior, and the protection of face, both for oneself and for others.

Culture Smart! Singapore introduces the Western visitor to the rich and varied cultures and customs of Singapore's communities. It shows what motivates people, how they interact with each other and with outsiders, and tells you what to expect and how to behave in unfamiliar situations. In doing so, it offers you a fuller, more rounded experience of this fascinating society.

Key Facts

Official Name	Republic of Singapore	Singapore is a member of ASEAN.
Capital	Singapore City	On the southeast coast of the Island.
Area	244 sq miles (633 sq km), virtually all urban.	
Currency	Singapore Dollar	
Climate	Tropical, hot 73°–90°F (23°–32°C), humid and rainy all year.	There is a monsoon season from November to January.
Population	2002: 4.2 million; 19% nonresident.	
Ethnic Makeup	Chinese 77% Malay 14% Indian 8% Eurasian 1%	
Religion	Buddhism, Taoism, Islam, Hinduism, Sikhism, Christianity, Judaism	Freedom of religion is enshrined in the Constitution.
Official Languages	Chinese (Mandarin), Malay, Tamil, English	Malay is the national language. English is the language of administration and business.
Government	Parliamentary republic, ruled by the People's Action Party since independence. Head of State: President Sellapan Rama (SR) Nathan; Prime Minister: Goh Chok Tong.	Cabinet appointed by the prime minister and responsible to parliament. The president is elected by popular vote for six years. Elections to unicameral parliament held every five years.

Adult Literacy	98% male, 88% female	Literacy in 2 or more languages 56%
Family Makeup	Average number of children per family: 1.24 Infant mortality rate: 4 per 1000 births	Age structure: 0–14 years 17%; 15–64 years 76%; 65 years and over 7%. Population growth: 1.8% per annum resident; 9% nonresident. Life expectancy: 77 years male, 84 years female.
Economy	Most prosperous in Asia in terms of per capita GDP. Much of the economy is based on importing and reexporting and financial services.	Exports: electronics, manufactures, and chemicals. GDP growth rate flat in 2000–2002; picking up with 0.8% in 2003.
Media	Both local and international newspapers and television channels are available.	Restrictions sometimes apply where international newspapers and magazines are highly critical of the government or its policies.
Electricity	220–240 volts/ 50Hz	
Telephone	International country code: 65	
Time Difference	GMT + 8 hours	

chapter one

LAND & PEOPLE

Singapore is a small island state at the southern end of the Malay Peninsula. Separated by narrow straits from mainland Malaysia, and by the Straits of Malacca from Sumatra, one of the largest islands in the Indonesian archipelago, it is approximately 20 miles (32 km) long east–west and 12 miles (20 km) wide north–south. It consists of fifty-nine islands and has a population of 4.2 million people.

Singapore City, on the southeast coast of the island, is dominated by tall skyscrapers, some taller than the island's highest point, Bukit Timah Hill. The modern buildings contain smart offices, numerous hotels, and glamorous shops. Yet despite the predominance of buildings, great thought and effort have gone into keeping the city green. You are immediately aware of this on the drive into the city from the airport—the long, straight road is lined with colorful bougainvilleas and frangipani as well as travelers' palms and jacarandas. This is possibly the best drive from an airport into a capital city anywhere in the world, as these are usually rather nondescript, if not downright grim, stretches of highway in most countries.

CLIMATE

The climate is tropical. Situated just 5° north of the equator, Singapore is either hot and sticky or very hot and sticky all year round. The monsoon weather, which lasts from November to January, brings heavy rain and occasional flooding, but this does lower the temperature from 86°F (30°C) to 73°F (23°C). The hottest and most humid months are from March to July—but expect dramatic thunderstorms at any time of the year. Be warned, though: many visitors catch cold, owing to the contrast of the outside temperature with the aggressive air-conditioning in some hotels and restaurants.

FLORA AND FAUNA

Singapore's national flower is the purple and white orchid "Vanda Miss Joaquim," a natural hybrid discovered in the garden of the lady of that name and subsequently presented to the Botanical Gardens. You will see the national emblem everywhere, from tourist trinkets and politicians' shirts to the carefully packed bunches on sale at the airport for travelers to take back to colder climes as a souvenir of exotic Southeast Asia. Singapore exports large quantities of these flowers, and the Mandai Orchid Gardens, with over two hundred species, are well worth a visit, as are the Singapore Botanic Gardens. These gardens make up the oldest public park in Singapore and are famous for being the birthplace of the region's rubber industry. This brought great wealth to the area—to Malaya for growing it and to the port of Singapore for its export.

There is a nature reserve at Bukit Timah Hill. This is Singapore's last remaining pocket of primary rain forest, and has an abundance of plant species. It is also the location of the island's highest point. Many visitors like to stroll to the peak to see the monkeys; this is best done either in the cool of the early morning or in the evening, avoiding the hottest times of the day.

Similarly, the best time to visit the Sungei Buloh Wetland Reserve on the north coast is in the early morning. This protected wetland nature park becomes a stopover point from November to March for migrating birds from as far away as Eastern Siberia. You can observe the birds in their natural environment from hides.

THE PEOPLE

Singapore is a land of immigrants. Apart from small coastal communities, it was virtually uninhabited until the nineteenth century, when Britain turned it into a strategic naval and commercial staging post, triggering substantial immigration, particularly from China. More of a salad bowl than a melting pot, the resulting society is a model of multicultural harmony. Although the Chinese are by far the largest ethnic group, the Malays who make up just over 14 percent of the population,

and the Indians who form 7 percent, contribute more to Singaporean society than their numbers would suggest.

The official languages of Singapore are therefore Malay (which is also the "national" language), Chinese (Mandarin), Tamil, and English. English is the language of administration, business, and technology.

The Chinese Immigrants

Life in China in the the last days of the Qing dynasty in the nineteenth century was harsh and oppressive for many. Poverty was widespread and those in the coastal provinces did not need much invitation to leave. The first junk bound for Singapore with migrants sailed from Amoy in 1821, and by 1827 the local Malay population was vastly outnumbered. The British encouraged this immigration, as the Chinese were reckoned to be a hardy and industrious people. Many were illiterate and penniless, but once they had paid off their passage they flourished. Some came as indentured laborers to work in the tin mines of Malaya and the docks in Singapore. They became coolies, farmers, and traders.

Their numbers continued to grow, even though the Singapore government tried to impose quotas, especially during the years of the Great Depression. The administration was always anxious to maintain a balance between the sexes and so avoid the problem of prostitution that had occurred in the early years of the nineteenth century when most of the immigrants were young men. In the early years of the twentieth century there were still more men than women: something like 240 men to every 100 women.

Most Overseas Chinese, not just those of Singapore, come from the southern coastal provinces between Hong Kong and Shanghai. Some were original inhabitants of the region and others had migrated south over the centuries. Although they are all Chinese, they come from a number of different ethnic groups. They share the same written language but speak completely different dialects and have different local cultures that they value.

However, most of these ethnic groups trace their origins to four river deltas: the Min River flows into the South China Sea at Fuzhou, the Chiu-lung at Xiamen (Amoy), the Han River near Shantou (Swatow), and the Pearl River south of Guangzhou (Canton) and opposite Hong Kong.

The people from Fuzhou speak Hokchiu; those from Xiamen speak Hokkien (this is the largest ethnic group in Singapore); those from Shantou speak Hoklo (but are called Teochew); and those from the Pearl River delta and Guangzhou call themselves and speak Cantonese. In the early days this led to factionalism and clan conflicts in Singapore.

The Hakka, who speak Hakka, emigrated from Guangdong, Fujian, and Jianxi provinces, and the Hainanese from Hainan Island, the most southerly part of China that is opposite the Vietnamese coast.

In Singapore today members of the older generation still speak their native dialects, but increasing numbers of young Chinese people speak Mandarin at home.

Straits Chinese

There was, however, a group of Chinese who came to settle in Singapore who were very different from the poor, illiterate migrants. They were the Straits Chinese, or Chinese who had adopted Malay customs. They were descendants of the old Chinese families of sixteenth-century Malacca and Penang. Over the centuries the Straits Chinese were influenced by their Malay neighbors, and some even felt more comfortable speaking Malay. The women adopted Malay-style dress and were referred to as Nonya. Their cuisine was transformed by typical Malay ingredients such as fragrant roots, herbs, chilies, and, above all, coconut milk. They combined the traditional love of pork—forbidden, of course, to Malay Muslims—with classic Malay ingredients.

The Straits Chinese were educated, had money, and soon found themselves an indispensable part of the colonial administration. Some became doctors, lawyers, and teachers, while others established successful businesses, especially in the timber and rubber trades. The men, referred to as the Baba community, were often ridiculed for being "more British than the British." Their newspapers were in English rather than Chinese, and they adopted the manners of their colonial masters, playing billiards and drinking brandy. Although they did not mix socially with the new Chinese immigrants, they kept abreast of developments on the mainland, especially those to do with the reform of Imperial China's archaic system of government, conducted by corrupt bureaucrats from northern China. So it comes as no surprise to learn that it was a Straits Chinese, Teo Eng Hock, who offered his large villa to Sun Yat Sen, the future first President of China, when he sought refuge in Singapore. You can visit his villa today and view its vast collection of artifacts and photographs, for the Singapore government restored the villa in 1964 to commemorate Sun Yat Sen and his revolutionary nationalist movement.

The Malay Community

The original Malay inhabitants of the island were soon outnumbered by the thousands of Chinese immigrants looking for a better way of life. It is a testament to the strength of their community that not only did it survive intact, but in many ways it influenced the newcomers. Malay is the national language of Singapore, and one of the four official languages. (English, however, is the language of administration.)

The Malays are a gentle, courteous people—always generous and hospitable. Indeed, together with the promotion of social harmony, these are core Malay values. They have a strong belief in community, no doubt growing out of the traditional *kampong* (small village) way of life. Although the *kampongs* have been replaced by the ethnically diverse Housing Development Blocks, their values still prevail.

The Malays have become self-reliant and have prospered in the new Singapore, owning apartments and holding down good jobs. They do not believe in the pursuit of wealth for its own sake, but in the greater importance of the spiritual side of life. This is reflected in their concern not only for their families but for their neighbors as well.

The Malays want visitors to enjoy Singapore and their particular Malay culture. However, there are still a few "dos and don'ts" that visitors should be aware of, which in turn will make them feel comfortable and not worry about upsetting or embarrassing their hosts. These are discussed in Chapter 4, The Singaporeans at Home, and Chapter 8, Business Briefing.

The Indian Community

Despite making up just over 7 percent of the population, Indians have always been prominent in politics and the law, possibly because they are passionate public speakers who love an argument. They are also well represented in the other professions, commerce, and industry.

To get an understanding of the Indian community it is a good idea to visit "Little India" on Serangoon Road. Some of the shops now have Chinese owners but still sell the traditional colorful wares that their customers demand. Indeed, most Indians still shop there, especially when buying saris, men's dhotis, betel nuts, heavy brass stands, garlands for weddings, arm bangles, and other indispensable items for an Indian household.

Like the Chinese, Indian shopkeepers appreciate a customer who will haggle and who relishes the prospect of a bargain. Again, as with the Chinese, the Indians regard it as a good omen if the first customer of the day buys something, however small, and especially if that purchase includes flowers, sugar, or sweets—but not oil. The latter is regarded as not a good sign for the rest of the day's trading.

SINGAPORE: A BRIEF HISTORY

Despite being such a new nation-state, Singapore has a long history, owing to its strategic position at the junction of many shipping routes. There is a mention in 203 CE in the writings of General Lu Tai of the Chinese Emperor's sending an

expedition to Pue-lo-Chung, as Singapore was then known. Much later, in the closing years of the thirteenth century, Marco Polo visited Sumatra and wrote about a noble city called Chiamassie, which historians have identified as Singapore. A hundred or so years later it had changed its name to Singapura, Sanskrit for "Lion City." Nobody knows why it got this name; the reason is lost in the mists of time. The city then went into decline as a result of the rivalry between the expanding Thai and Javanese empires. Singapore's geographical position, which was to be such a bonus six hundred years later, meant that it became a pawn in these internecine wars, and this led to its abandonment when the traders moved to Malacca, which was fortified and much more secure. Only a few people—known as sea people—remained, surviving on fishing and, when times were hard, piracy.

Early Days

Long before the British arrived the location was favored by traders taking their wares from Arabia, India, and the Malay peninsula to East and Southeast Asia and back again on the seasonal monsoon winds. This activity reached a peak as a port under the Malays in the thirteenth century, but was later curtailed by the Mongols and so it remained until the arrival of Raffles.

Colonization

In the eighteenth century Britain and the Netherlands were commercial competitors in the East-West trade, while Britain and France were military enemies and sought to extend their empires in the region. Early in the nineteenth century the French were defeated in Europe and no longer posed a threat to British and Dutch interests in Asia. The British and the Dutch then set out to acquire exclusive trading posts through agreements with local rulers.

Britain was represented in the region by the powerful East India Company whose commercial strength was backed by its own military force. It had long wanted to have a halfway house between Bengal, its power base, and Canton, the source of its new wealth in tea and the destination for its opium, produced in India, for which the Company had a monopoly. The Dutch were snapping up what seemed the best ports, and Thomas, later Sir Stamford, Raffles of the Company had long wanted to establish a trading post in the region. "Our object is not territory but trade," he wrote, "a great commercial emporium and a fulcrum whence we may extend our influence politically as circumstances may hereafter require." He negotiated a treaty with Sultan Hussein of Johore giving Britain the right to establish a trading post on the island of Singapore and proclaim it a free port, and on February 6, 1819, the Union flag of Great Britain was officially raised. Security and stability soon attracted ships in search of a safe haven to restock with food and water and those needing to repair their vessels. Success was almost guaranteed.

Raffles was one of a special breed of freewheeling and adventurous spirits produced by Britain's great commercial empire. However else one views it today, the Empire gave opportunities and scope to many British men of humble birth, many of whom became efficient and fair administrators, humanitarian in their outlook and practical in their approach.

Raffles (1781–1826)

Thomas Stamford Raffles was born on a slave ship (his father was the Captain) in the mid Atlantic. He was forced to leave school at the age of fourteen when his father could no longer afford the fees. However, he was fortunate enough to obtain a clerical position in the East India Company in 1805, and ten years later he was on his way to Penang in northwestern Malaya to take up a position as Assistant Secretary in the Government. Raffles was ambitious and used his time wisely on the voyage out by learning Malay. He was soon considered fluent, and by 1811 his hard work paid off and he was appointed Governor of Java. After a spell back in England and a second marriage, his first wife, Olivia, having died in 1814, he was appointed Governor of Sumatra. In 1818 he persuaded the Governor General of India, Lord Hastings, to agree to an expedition to set up a trading post at the southern tip of Malacca.

Although his name is forever linked with Singapore, Raffles (he dropped the "Thomas" when knighted by the Prince Regent) spent surprisingly little time in the trading post. However, he took a keen interest in his project, and after each visit he left clear instructions as to the layout and development of the city. He stipulated that the streets be laid out in a grid pattern and that the houses conform to a specified style with a veranda and covered passages to ameliorate the climate. He later divided the area into *kampongs* (the Malay word for village) and promoted the education of the native Malay population. As in Java, Raffles was interested in the welfare of local people and set up wise and compassionate rule.

His life, like that of many others who lived in the tropics, including his children, was cut short prematurely. He returned to England in 1824, and two years later he died of a brain tumor. Before his death he was instrumental in the founding of the first Zoological Gardens in the world in London; he is also remembered as a great friend of William Wilberforce and the antislavery movement.

Although barely remembered in the land of his birth, Sir Stamford Raffles is not forgotten in Singapore. First came a bronze statue, saved during the Japanese occupation and once again proudly on display, and then came a magnificent hotel, bearing his name, which has been a byword for luxury for many decades.

Development

British political control went hand in hand with trade and Singapore continued to flourish in the nineteenth century. In 1826 the island was combined with Penang and Malacca to form the Straits Settlements, ruled by the Governor of Bengal. In 1832 Singapore became the capital of the Straits Settlements; its port prospered and attracted Chinese and Indian immigrants. In 1851 the Straits Settlements became the responsibility of the Governor General of India. In 1858 the administration was run directly from London through the India Office, and in 1867 the Straits Settlements became a Crown Colony of the British Empire.

Economically Singapore grew from strength to strength, especially after the development of the rubber industry in Malaya and the opening of the Suez Canal in 1869. Western investments, banking, and business practices brought their advantages. The end of the century saw Singapore

at the hub of international trade in the region.
While the Malays resented and periodically
rebelled against the British, Singapore remained
calm and thrived as the area's primary port for the
export of rubber and tin. The British authorities
opened English-language primary schools, while
the Chinese majority built Chinese-language
schools.

Singapore was largely unaffected by the First
World War, but after the war there was a dramatic
rise in tin and rubber prices and this created great
wealth for some. The strategic military
importance of the island became more apparent
as the British defended their colonial empire and
in 1922 it became the principal British military
base in East Asia. Anti-Japanese sentiment among
the Chinese population grew after Japan invaded
Manchuria in 1931 and British officials outlawed
anti-Japanese demonstrations and propaganda.

Japanese Occupation

Japan invaded the Malay Peninsula in December
1941 and barely three months later the British
surrendered Singapore. The occupation of
"Syonan," as the Japanese named Singapore, was
brutal and savage. Thousands of expatriates,
including women and children, were rounded up
and put into camps for the duration of the War.
Many never survived the starvation, disease, and

cruel punishments, as was the case with many thousands of Allied prisoners of war. Others were tortured and imprisoned in the notorious Changi jail. What is often forgotten, though, is that some 50,000 Chinese men between the ages of eighteen and fifty, labeled "undesirables" by the Japanese, were arrested and summarily executed. In Esplanade Park you can see the monument to Lim Bo Seng, a prominent Chinese businessman and resistance fighter. He was arrested by the dreaded Kempeitai, the Japanese Secret Police, and, despite months of torture, he refused to betray his comrades. His family also paid with their lives. Near the causeway linking Singapore with Malaysia is the War Memorial to the Allied troops stationed in Southeast Asia during the Second World War who died at Fort Siloso on Sentosa Island. Also on the island is the Wax Works Museum with tableaux depicting both the fall of Singapore in 1942 and the formal surrender by Japanese forces on August 14, 1945. This momentous event ended one of the most painful periods in Singapore's history.

Many older Singaporeans, however, have long memories and find it difficult to forget and, especially, to forgive. Like China and Korea, Singapore is still demanding that Japanese history textbooks state clearly what took place during the

occupation of these countries. So far their
demands have fallen on deaf ears.

Understandably the younger generation takes a
more pragmatic view, realizing that the world has
greatly changed in the last sixty years. They
welcome Japanese investment and technology, as
well as the large number of Japanese tourists who
visit, spending freely in the department stores,
bazaars, restaurants, and hotels.

Independence

After the War, Singapore's fortunes were
inextricably bound up with those of Malaya, but
despite calls for a unified Malay Peninsula Britain
resisted, although it became a separate Crown
Colony in 1946. In the early 1950s the
government of Singapore consisted of a British-
appointed governor and a legislative council
whose members were mostly wealthy Chinese
businessmen. This introduced primary education
in Singapore's four main languages. This was
followed by a period in which the pressure for
self-rule grew, but with student and labor unrest
Britain was reluctant to cede control. However,

Singapore became self-
governing in 1959 with
Lee Kuan Yew of the
People's Action Party
(PAP) being elected as

Prime Minister at the age of thirty-five. He was in favor of a federation with Malaya. Lee introduced a new flag, a new national anthem, and made English, Chinese, Malay, and Tamil the official languages. Four years later, when Malaya gained its independence, Singapore joined the newly created Federation of Malaysia.

Over the decades the Chinese had worked hard, assumed managerial positions, and prospered, not only in Malaya but also in Singapore. This led to resentment by the Malays. From the beginning there were political and racial tensions in the Federation, not least of which were  the concerns expressed by the Malay states that the power and influence of the largely Chinese population of Singapore would dominate the new Federation. After much agonizing and wrangling, Singapore was expelled, and on August 9, 1965, the Lion City became an independent republic. August 9 is now a National Holiday

Lee promised to create honest government and a single multicultural national identity, and to expand trade. He fostered good relations with his neighbors so that in 1967 Singapore joined Indonesia, Malaysia, the Philippines, and Thailand in the regional Association of Southeast Asian Nations (ASEAN).

LEE KUAN YEW

Lee Kuan Yew was born in Singapore in 1923, a third-generation descendant of immigrants from Guangdong province. He studied law at Cambridge University, England, and in 1954 he formed the People's Action Party (PAP).

It has to be said that it was Lee's personal vision, energy, and drive that made Singapore into the Asian powerhouse that it is today. Within a few years of independence the economy grew, manufacturing prospered, and the port facilities—its deep-water harbor was Singapore's only natural asset—soon rivaled those of London and New York, as it was strategically placed to be the distribution center for the rest of Asia.

Unlike many other countries in the region, the wealth from the rapid economic growth filtered down to the poorest in society. Lee was determined that obedience to the rule of law would stifle corruption—something that still bedevils the region. He also believed passionately in equality of opportunity, no matter what one's ethnic origins were.

Lee's vision of a prosperous, multiracial society has paid off handsomely: Singapore has a highly educated population, one of the highest literacy rates in the world, and excellent health care, social security, and transportation systems. Many citizens own their own homes in the brightly colored high-rise apartment blocks of the Housing Development Board (HDB).

Although Lee Kuan Yew officially retired in 1990 to assume the post of senior minister in the Singapore cabinet, no one doubts that his influence over the ruling PAP remains.

SOCIAL CHANGE

At the time of independence the social makeup of society could be described as a Chinese majority, which, while represented in all strata of society, dominated politics and government; Malays worked in the civil service, as policemen, servants, or laborers, and Indians were often shopkeepers or laborers.

Unfortunately the vision of a multiethnic society was not easy to achieve and in 1964-5, prior to the expulsion from the Federation of Malaysia, tension between the Chinese and the Malay underclass population boiled over. Fomented by extremist groups from Kuala Lumpur, race riots between Malay and Chinese youths led to deaths.

Following independence the government set out to free up the labor market by passing laws that gave employers more hiring and firing power; but workers saw changes, too, and for the first time received sick leave and unemployment benefits. Birthrates rose, and the Family Planning and Population Board began to offer clinical services, education, and incentives such as priority housing and education in exchange for voluntary sterilization.

The Housing Development Board
To raise living conditions and break down ethnic

barriers, the new Housing Development Board (HDB) built high-rise apartment complexes and relocated lower-income citizens. The complexes featured schools, shops, and recreation areas. Many families used their compulsory contributions to the Central Provident Fund to buy apartments. Legislative support came in the form of the Land

Acquisition Act set up in 1967 to compulsorily acquire private land for public housing or other development programs. Together with sensitive resettlement policies, this Act enabled the HDB to clear squatters and slum areas smoothly and in their place build new and comfortable HDB apartments. In the process the environment went from Third World squalor to First World standards. Today, about 85 percent of Singaporeans live in HDB flats compared with only 9 percent in 1960 when the HDB was first established. The government supports this public housing program by providing financial assistance for the funding of housing development and other activities. This is one of the few successful examples of the great modernist architect Le Corbusier's dream of the high-density city of the future.

The Central Development Fund

Singapore's compulsory social security savings scheme, the Central Provident Fund (CPF), was founded in 1955 and is an important engine of social change. Originally employees deposited a predetermined portion of their income into a tax-exempt account, which the employer matched. Today the rate of contribution is variable, and this adjustment is used by the government as an economic regulatory tool. The CPF is a comprehensive savings plan that has provided many working Singaporeans with a sense of security and confidence in their old age. Its overall scope and benefits encompass retirement, health care, home ownership, family protection, and asset enhancement.

CPF savings earn interest. Savings in the Ordinary Account earn a minimum interest rate of 2.5 percent per annum, while savings in the Special Savings for old age contingencies and

Medisave Accounts earn additional interest of 1.5 percentage points above the prevailing Ordinary Account interest rate. The most significant social outcome of the CPF is that most Singaporeans are able to own their own homes.

In the 1970s emphasis on education raised living standards, reduced poverty, and blurred class lines. Most families occupied, and many owned, HDB apartments. The command of English and technical or professional skills marked the upwardly mobile.

The 1980s saw a growing need for manpower and the state responded by expanding vocational training and encouraging more women to work. An important element of this recruitment drive was the education of women. This transformed the workplace, and today Singapore is unique in Asia in terms of women's presence and position in the workforce. While this policy boosted household incomes, it had the unwelcome consequence of further lowering the birthrate, and the government launched a pro-birth campaign, offering tax rebates and day care subsidies for the third child.

To ensure a balanced racial mix within HDB estates and to foster greater racial harmony, the ethnic integration policy was introduced. Even today, the HDB continues with its community builder role by working with other government ministries to provide social facilities such as community centers and neighborhood parks. Towns are planned with precinct spaces such as amphitheaters and pavilions to give residents more opportunities to interact with one another for a more cohesive community.

The 1990s were marked by the troubles in Indonesia and this led to more unskilled refugees arriving. A sign of a maturing economy was the departure of some members of Singapore's professional class for overseas opportunities.

LAW AND ORDER

The country's stability has come at a price. Many critics would argue that Singapore is over governed—a "managed democracy" with too many rules and strictures. Most visitors are surprised that heavy fines are levied on those who chew gum or spit in public places, jaywalk, or drop litter. Smoking is banned in most restaurants and there is a heavy fine for not flushing a public lavatory after use. As for vandalism, it is not only punished by a fine but, in some circumstances, the punishment is caning—

anything from three to eight strokes. There is no trial by jury. After independence it was initially retained for murder, but with too few convictions, in the view of the government, it was phased out.

In the 1980s the approach became softer and community policing was introduced and small neighborhood posts were opened. By the end of the decade 15 percent of police officers were women.

The 1990s saw the judiciary demonstrate its constitutional independence by ruling against the government in many political and civil rights cases. Although government officials intimidate political opponents and censor the press, they make no attempt to reverse rulings, or to remove or intimidate judges. Today Singapore remains a tightly ruled society, but maintains what it sees as a fair balance between openness and control.

POLITICAL LIFE

Despite the recent recession, the People's Action Party remains overwhelmingly dominant, thanks both to its own popularity and to the harsh measures to limit opposition campaigning. It won eighty-four of the eighty-six seats in the 2001 general election.

The authoritarian style of Lee Kuan Yew and his successor Goh Chok Tong has all but suppressed political opposition. Life is made very difficult for those who oppose the PAP; there is little political debate in the media and many parliamentary candidates are returned to power without opposition. While much of this may seem oppressive to the Western visitor, it is worth remembering that for more than thirty years the PAP rule has meant wise, efficient government. The people's standard of living has steadily improved, with Singapore having the highest rate of home ownership and national savings in the world, coupled with respect for law and order. This is a multiracial society that lives in harmony.

Discussing these matters with Singaporeans is not recommended, as the government is sensitive to criticism by foreigners. Furthermore, Lee Kuan Yew and his successors feel that the West has given up on its own values—pointing to drug abuse, crime, and violence in Western society and the associated breakdown of family life and homelessness. If a Singaporean does venture any views on politics, the comment will probably be that politics is best left to the politicians, while ordinary people get on with the important business of making money.

For some young people, though, this heavily managed society can lead to problems when they leave it. There is, admittedly anecdotal, evidence to suggest that some of those who leave to study in the West find the unexpected and exhilarating

freedoms of New York, London, Sydney, or
Vancouver difficult to handle.

LOW POPULATION GROWTH

Singapore's society is changing in one dramatic
way, and that is in the worrying decline in the
birthrate. In the period 1990–2000 the resident
population growth has been only 1.8 percent per
annum, well short of the number needed for it to
replace itself. Ever since the 1980s the
government has been aware of the demographic
time bomb and has rigorously pursued a pro-
natal policy, without much success.

Many women are delaying the age at which
they marry and have children because they wish
to pursue careers, and there are very few social
services for working mothers. Lee Kuan Yew is
supposed to have declared that he regretted
giving women equal educational and
employment opportunities in the 1960s, and the
present prime minister, Goh Chok Tong, has
brought in more and more incentives for women
to have larger families, echoing the 1980s slogan
of "go for three or more." The difference
nowadays, though, is that the government pays
bonuses to those who do. Of course, Singapore
could again look to immigrants to keep its
population growing, but as prime minister Goh

recently stated, "…but they cannot replace us," as not all the new arrivals share the same cultural values and attitudes to conformity as the present population.

The government has even taken to desperate measures such as launching a "Romancing Singapore" campaign on Valentine's Day to bring singles together by sponsoring rock-climbing trips and love-boat cruises, and setting up dating agencies so that well-educated female graduates can have the opportunity to meet prospective partners.

chapter two

VALUES & ATTITUDES

COMMON ASIAN VALUES

The island state is home to three of Asia's great cultures: Chinese, Malay, and Indian and, although they each have their own distinct norms, values, and religions, many of these are held in common. So a Singaporean Chinese, Malay, and Indian will share much more with each other than with any Westerner. Perhaps this explains in part why Singapore has become such a successful multicultural society.

For instance, a group's or an individual's dignity is to be respected at all times, and anything that undermines it is totally taboo. The "loss of face," in other words anything that severely embarrasses the group or individual, must be avoided at all costs. Furthermore all three ethnic groups, while strongly believing in equality of opportunity, also firmly believe in a hierarchical society, one that gives deference to age and learning, where status is earned and not simply inherited, and where position in turn brings responsibility.

   Relationships are important and have to be worked at over a long period of time. Singaporeans therefore prefer to do business with people they know, such as family and friends, or school and university contacts. Thus, when there are problems, businesses first look to their suppliers and customers for help rather than to the contract and their lawyers, as is often the case in the West.

   Outside a business context, Singaporeans can be synchronic in their approach to time, and they consider social time commitments to be desirable rather than important. One thing at a time is not the order of the day; instead many things are done at once and time is elastic. With this goes the habit of changing details and plans frequently. Westerners who focus on the arrangement rather than the relationship will often find this frustrating.

   Perhaps because of these values, the Singaporeans can seem indirect and ambiguous in their approach, compared to Westerners, who have a way of speaking directly and saying what is on their minds. Singaporeans do not want to upset or embarrass anyone by disagreeing, and so an affirmative answer or reply might not mean anything more than "I hear you." Similarly, Singaporeans will not usually be direct when giving bad news—they are not setting out to deceive, but they do not want to upset the hearer or damage the relationship.

RELIGION

Singapore is a secular state that rightly prides itself on its religious tolerance, and its citizens are free to worship as they see fit. In fact, religion plays an important role in society and everyday life. To a great extent the different ethnic communities are defined by their religion, and many of their characteristic values, attitudes, and customs are rooted in traditional belief.

The Chinese

To the Chinese, religion is first and foremost about easing their passage through this difficult life. Their belief system is a pragmatic combination of three quite different religious philosophies—Taoism, Buddhism, and Confucianism. Taken together, these address a range of spiritual, intellectual, and social needs, and have sustained the Chinese people for thousands of years.

Unsurprisingly, the Singaporean Chinese have not been influenced in the matter of religion, as they have in cuisine, by their Muslim Malay neighbors. Perhaps it had something to do with the strictures against drinking alcohol and the eating of certain foods beloved by the Chinese, such as pork. Although some Chinese have converted to Christianity, especially the Protestant evangelical sects, this is an immense step for them and their families. Chinese parents and grandparents are greatly alarmed that their newly converted Christian sons and daughters and their descendants will no longer be able to carry out funeral rites, and especially the worship and veneration of the ancestors.

Taoism

Taoism is essentially about living in harmony with the natural world. The Chinese word *tao* means "way." It sees the universe as being divided into two opposing yet complementary aspects, the primal forces of Yin and Yang. These polarities are illustrated by the Yin-Yang symbol. The two swirling shapes inside the circle give the impression of change—the only constant factor in the universe. One tradition states that Yin (or Ying, the dark side) represents the breath that formed the earth. Yang (the light side) symbolizes the breath that formed the heavens. The most common view is that Yin represents aspects of the feminine, being soft, cool, calm, introspective, and healing, and Yang the masculine, being hard, hot, energetic, moving, and sometimes aggressive. Another view has Yin representing the night and Yang the day. However, since nothing in nature is purely black or white, the symbol includes a small black spot in the white swirl, and a corresponding white spot in the black swirl. Each state contains the seed of its opposite.

This principle of balancing forces is embedded in Chinese thought. Everything must be in balance—in the world, the nation, and the human body—for it to prosper. According to this belief, a root cause of illness in the body is the imbalance between Yin (cool) and Yang (hot) foods. Similarly, traditional relationships must be kept harmonious, for example, between father and son, husband and wife, a ruler and his subjects, and between nation-state and nation-state. In this way Taoism, although itself an irreverent and quietist philosophy, can complement the conservative rigidity of Confucian teaching.

Chinese belief embraces a panoply of deities,

ghosts, and devils, and temples are sited and built strictly according to the rules of Feng Shui, so that they will be free from evil. Feng Shui, the ancient art of geomancy, holds that the proper alignment of walls, furniture, and objects will greatly enhance the flow of *chi*—energy, or the life force—and bring prosperity to the prudent occupants of the building or the worshipers at the temple. The visitor to a Chinese temple will be aware of this as he has to step over a curb that is supposed to trip up evil spirits, and then pass through doors painted with images of terrifying gods and guarded by two lions, female and male, representing Yin and Yang. When stepping into the inner courtyard the visitor is obliged to remove his shoes. Although the Chinese are reverential when visiting their temples, they also see them as places where the community can come together, to meet, to exchange ideas, and maybe to gossip amid the chants, gongs, and bells, and the perfumed smell of incense.

Buddhism

Buddhism addresses the problem of human suffering and finds a way to resolve it. Its founder, Siddhartha Gautama, the Buddha (or "Enlightened One"), was born a Hindu prince in about 563 BCE in what today is Nepal. His teachings spread far beyond India to flourish and

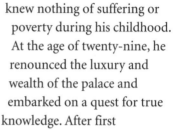

grow in China, Korea, Japan, and Southeast Asia. Born into great wealth, Siddhartha Gautama knew nothing of suffering or poverty during his childhood. At the age of twenty-nine, he renounced the luxury and wealth of the palace and embarked on a quest for true knowledge. After first embracing extreme ascetic practices, he reverted to "the middle way" of meditation until, at the age of thirty-four, seated beneath a banyan, or bo, tree he experienced enlightenment.

Buddha was originally reacting against the excesses of the Brahmin priests whom he had seen lusting after wealth and power, which lead to unhappiness both in this life and the next. He taught that in order to attain *nirvana*, or true enlightenment, one had first to recognize the Four Noble Truths. They are that life is suffering; there is a cause of suffering—our attachment to notions and things; there is an end to suffering—our attachment is, in essence, empty; and that the way to achieve the end of suffering is by following the Eightfold Path. This depends on right thought or view, right intention, right speech, right action, right livelihood, right effort, right mindfulness, and right *samadhi* or concentration.

Buddhism later split into two major schools: Theravada ("teaching of the elders")—also known, pejoratively, as Hinayana (or "lesser vehicle")—which teaches individuals how to attain personal enlightenment; and Mahayana (the "greater vehicle"), which teaches the Great Compassion—the practitioner delays his own *nirvana* until all other beings have been liberated. Both strands of Buddhism are present in Singapore, although the latter is more popular.

Confucian Philosophy

Not so much a religion as an ethical system, the philosophy of Confucianism has shaped Chinese civilization for over two thousand years. The scholar-sage Confucius was born in around 551 BCE. He devoted his life to the study and teaching of the Chinese classics, and his writings are mainly comments on these. The origin of things lies in the union of Yin and Yang. Human relationships are hierarchical. Confucius emphasized personal virtue, promotion on merit by scholarship, devotion to the family, and justice. His precepts dealt with morality in human affairs, and continue to form a practical guide for the daily life of people. They include obedience to authority, adherence to one's social position, respect for the elderly, and the veneration of ancestors. They also stress the virtues of education, hard work, thrift, loyalty, and harmony. Unlike contemporary Western value systems, Confucianism does not give overriding importance to the rights of the individual; it stresses the needs of the group, and the duties and obligations of the individual.

CONFUCIUS' FIVE BASIC RELATIONSHIPS IN SOCIETY

Sovereign – Subject

Father – Son

Husband – Wife

Elder Brother – Younger Brother
(Elder Sister – Younger Sister)

Friend – Friend

Confucianism in Practice

From infancy onward Chinese children know that they belong to a tightly knit group and they are taught never to dishonor the group or bring shame upon it. If a member of the family needs help, whether it is financial or moral, the rest of the family will come to his or her aid. Taking in orphaned nieces or nephews, rescuing a brother or sister from bankruptcy, and supporting a family member who is sick and unemployed are all part of family obligation. The child who places his or her needs ahead of others is considered to be amoral, untrustworthy, and something of a social misfit!

These Confucian values, first taught in the home, are later reinforced at school, often in a practical manner—such as designating a group to be responsible for books for the whole class, or serving the rest of the children at lunch, or clearing up after lunch or at the end of the school day.

Obligation comes in many forms, but none more so than in the case of care for elderly parents. For the adult child, especially the eldest son, knows that it was his parents who gave him and his siblings the gift of life, and thereafter love and nurture. So it is the child's responsibility to attend to the needs of his parents, providing them with shelter (it used to be the norm in Singapore that three generations would live under one roof, but this is less the case now) and the wherewithal to enjoy a contented old age, free from want and safe in the knowledge that after their deaths the correct mourning procedures, and the veneration due to them, would be carried out.

Education is highly valued, not only because it ensures a good career and, hopefully, a prosperous one, but because it is essential for the development of individual potential, which enhances the whole group.

Singapore is most definitely not an "I" society. How very different from Western cultures where rugged individualism and self-assertiveness are encouraged from an early age. Likewise, countries in the West generally promote egalitarian ideals and disapprove of status and hierarchy, although in reality we often see them in practice! Asian societies have no such qualms, and indeed encourage the paying of respect to people of higher status, whether it means venerating age, because of the wisdom it has brought, or learning, because of the long years of study needed to achieve a particular professional position. Similarly, the boss is looked up to in a Singaporean company and expects loyalty from his staff. In return he is expected to take a paternalistic interest in their family as well as work-related problems.

The government has harnessed Confucianism to create a more cohesive society, encouraging the three-tier family, filial piety, and education.

Young People

It is not too difficult to see that Confucian values would create a dedicated, highly motivated, and responsible workforce with an enhanced sense of commitment and loyalty. It is also true to say, however, that some young Singaporeans think that these values are no longer relevant in the modern world. In fact, the government became so concerned by this trend that it carried out a

survey to find out what young Singaporeans
thought were important values today.
Reassuringly, the overwhelming majority stated
that filial piety, honesty, responsibility, and self
control were as important to them as they had
been to their ancestors.

The Malays

Something like 99 percent of the Malay
population in Singapore is Muslim. This was not
always the case, as Buddhism and Hinduism were
the earliest religious influences, but by the time
Marco Polo visited Southeast Asia in 1292,
Islam was well established, with mosques being
built on the sites of former Buddhist and Hindu
temples.

Islam

Islam was the last of the world's great religions to
be founded. The word *Islam* means "entering into
a condition of peace and security with God
through allegiance or surrender
to him." The religion teaches
the acceptance of and
obedience to the word of
God as finally revealed to the
prophet Muhammad. Born in
idol-worshiping Mecca in the Arabian Peninsula
c. 570 CE, Muhammad received the call in midlife

to proclaim the worship of one God (Allah) in about 616. He established the first Islamic community in Medina after fleeing persecution in Mecca. Today both cities are holy to Muslims.

The holy book of Islam, recording the uncorrupted word of God revealed to Muhammad by the angel Gabriel, is the Koran (*Quran*). It contains a clear code of conduct governing aspects of daily life, such as dressing modestly, and forbids the drinking of alcohol, the eating of pork and certain other foods, and gambling. The second-most important source of Islamic teaching is the Hadith ("tradition"), which forms a commentary on the Koran. The fundamental duties that shape Muslim life are called the Five Pillars of the Faith.

THE FIVE PILLARS OF ISLAM

Affirmation: the duty to recite the creed "There is no God but Allah, and Muhammad is the Messenger of God."

Prayer: the duty to worship God in prayer five times each day.

Almsgiving: the duty to distribute alms and to help the needy.

Fasting: self-purification and the duty to keep the fast of Ramadan.

Pilgrimage: the duty to make the pilgrimage, or *Hajj*, to the shrine of the Ka'aba at Mecca at least once in a lifetime.

It is always a good idea for the visitor to be aware of the month of Ramadan, the ninth month in the lunar calendar, as all good Muslims, apart from the elderly, the very young, pregnant women, and nursing mothers, are expected to fast. No food or drink may be taken between sunrise and sunset. Although the fast is seen as beneficial to health, it is regarded principally as a method of spiritual self-purification. By cutting oneself off from worldly comforts, even for a short time, a fasting person gains true sympathy with those who go hungry, as well as growth in his or her spiritual life. Therefore it would be the height of insensitivity to eat in the presence of someone you knew to be a Muslim, whether Indian or Malay, at this time.

It is forbidden for Muslim men and women to touch members of the opposite sex outside the immediate family, so do not automatically go to shake the hand of a female colleague. Certain animals, such as pigs, dogs, and amphibians are considered unclean, so if you invite Malay friends to your house and you have pet dogs, it is a good idea to put them in another room for the duration of the visit. Remember a Muslim is strictly forbidden to come into contact with the nose, saliva, or hair of a dog.

Friday is the Muslim day of prayer, and you will see people making their way to the mosques dressed in their best clothes for the occasion. Malay men traditionally wear black velvet hats, or *songkoks*. Commerce and industry accommodate Muslim devotions on Friday by arranging a specially long lunch hour from about 11:30 a.m. in the morning to 2:30 p.m. in the afternoon.

Non-Muslims are allowed to visit mosques providing they are quiet and respectful and remember to take their shoes off before entering. Visitors should be modestly dressed, and women especially should have their arms, legs, and head covered. Of course, you should always ask permission before taking any photographs. A good time to visit is between 9:00 a.m. and 12 noon, when the mosque is relatively quiet.

Budi

Malays also have their own philosophical code of behavior, which is similar in some respects to Confucianism. This is known as Budi. According to its laws the individual should always have a pleasant disposition, should show respect for other people, especially older people, and should always be courteous toward them. To show love and affection toward one's parents is also important, as is the maintenance of harmony in the family and society as a whole.

The Indians

The Indian community, unlike the Malay community, is not defined by one religion. Over half its members are Hindu, but others are Muslim, others Sikh, while others—especially those from Southern India—are Christian.

Hinduism

Hinduism originated in North India about four thousand years ago. Superficially it embraces many apparent contradictions, differing forms of worship, and a profusion of divinities. Underlying this wide variety, however, there is unity. Hindus believe in one God: Brahman the supreme, ultimate reality, whose many manifestations are depicted in a wealth of images. As long as a Hindu identifies himself with the Hindu faith, accepts as sacred the ancient Vedic literature, and recognizes the caste system, he is assured a place in Hindu society.

Hinduism has several sacred works, the oldest of which are the Vedic scriptures, the tales, songs, and ceremonial instructions of the Indo-European Aryan settlers in the Indian subcontinent. There are four *Vedas* (Sanskrit for "knowledge"): the *Rig Veda*, probably the oldest religious book in the world, compiled between 1500 BCE and 900 BCE; the *Sama Veda*, a collection of sacred songs; the *Yajur Veda*, the text used by priests in the performance of their religious duties; and the *Atharva Veda*, a book of incantations. These, together with the great Hindu Epics, the *Ramayana* and the *Mahabharata*—the tales of early Aryan heroes, the most famous of which is the *Bhagavad Gita*—contain the basic beliefs of modern Hinduism.

Hindus believe that all living beings have souls. Life is a series of rebirths and reincarnations until the soul, by its virtuous behavior, is released from the cycle of birth and death. An individual's spiritual progress is determined by *karma* (the law of consequence, or fate), and by *dharma* (the obligation to accept one's condition and perform the duties appropriate to it). As no one can escape the duties of *dharma*, this naturally reinforces the Indian caste system. These duties are prescribed by the Hindu priest or Brahmin. Hindus therefore believe that in this life they get what they deserve; whatever happens, it is the consequence of behavior in one's previous lives. Personal duty is all-important in the Hindu faith.

The Hindu trinity symbolizes the three aspects of Brahman. Brahma is the creator, Vishnu the preserver or sustainer, and Shiva the completer or destroyer. There are also many other gods and goddesses in the Hindu pantheon. One of the most popular is Ganesh, the elephant god. He is the god of good luck, and no undertaking, apart from funerals, is contemplated without involving and making an offering to him.

EDUCATION

Education is highly regarded in Asian societies. In Singapore, however, the introduction of free compulsory education has transformed the social scene. Government reforms first raised educational standards in all state schools and narrowed the gap in attainment between different social groups. Now private educational establishments are being introduced, with subsidies to keep them accessible. The universities, too, are heavily subsidized. The general high standard of education has created more opportunities for all, and this has changed attitudes. While Singapore is still in many ways a traditionally hierarchical Asian society, in the last thirty years merit has come very much to the fore, and the country prides itself on being a meritocracy.

A GOAL-DRIVEN SOCIETY

A consequence of the wider opportunities now available is that younger Singaporeans of all ethnic backgrounds prize success. In the workplace this can lead to a more goal-oriented approach, rather than the traditional relationship-based dealings of their parents. Socially, perhaps, it can be seen in that uniquely Singaporean form of status anxiety known as *kiasu*—literally, this means "fear of losing," or, in other words, missing out. If your neighbor is hurrying out to the shops to buy the latest piece of electronic wizardry, then you had better rush to do so too, in case there won't be any left. You don't want to be lagging behind. "*Kiasu*" is a word that the traveler will often hear. Because their country is so new and so prosperous, Singaporeans love to indulge in a bit of navel-gazing—it is not only the visitor who wants to know what makes Singapore tick. So do they themselves.

chapter three

CUSTOMS &
TRADITIONS

FESTIVALS AND HOLIDAYS

If you like festivals and celebrations you will love
Singapore. At any given time, thanks to the many
different ethnic groups, there is likely to be a
festival in progress. The main events are Chinese
New Year and the Hungry Ghosts festival, the
Hindu Deepavali, the Festival of Lights, the
Muslim Hari Raya Puasa, the celebration that
ends the fast of Ramadan, and Christmas. Some
festivals are also public holidays.

PUBLIC HOLIDAYS	
New Year's Day	1 January
Chinese New Year	January or February*
Hari Raya Haji	January*
Good Friday	Around April*
Labor Day	1 May
Vesak Day	April, May, or June*
Singapore National Day	9 August
Deepavali	October or November*
Hari Raya Puasa	End of Ramadan*
Christmas Day	25 December

* Dates vary according to the different lunar calendars.

Chinese New Year

The Chinese New Year, also known as the Lunar New Year, begins on the second new moon after the winter solstice, usually between mid January and mid February, and lasts fifteen days. Everyday life on the island seems to come to a halt for the duration. The festival is preceded by a flurry of household activity: cleaning, to sweep out bad luck, cooking special regional foods of mainland China, plus shopping trips for new clothes. The celebration proper starts on New Year's Eve, when families are invited to a grand reunion dinner at the paternal home, and children pay respects to their parents. Candles burn all night and homage is paid to the ancestors. The evening's activities reaffirm the family's identity and closeness. The noisy part begins at midnight, when drums and kettles are banged (firecrackers have now been banned) and windows are thrown open to usher out the old and usher in the New Year.

Next morning it is the custom for children to serve their parents tea, and they in turn give them *Hong Bao*, red envelopes containing money. Family and friends visit each other over the next few days, except for the third day, which is dedicated to remembering and venerating the ancestors. On the fourth day businessmen usually hold a grand banquet for their employees.

Giving Hong Bao

Visiting foreigners who are married should know to give *Hong Bao* to their hosts' children. Also, during the Chinese New Year a foreign manager should give *Hong Bao* to his staff. Check with your colleagues on the appropriate amount.

The traditional procession marking the Chinese New Year has turned into Singapore's biggest street event. The carnival-like Chingay Parade features lion dances, acrobats, children, beauty queens, and cultural shows from different lands.

Vesak Day

This day, on the full moon of the fourth lunar month of the Indian calendar, in April, May, or June, commemorates the birth and enlightenment of the Buddha and his entry into *nirvana*. In

Singapore the various Buddhist sects celebrate Vesak Day in different ways. In the temples priests in saffron robes chant *sutras* while devotees pray, meditate, and make offerings. As an act of compassion, in accordance with the Buddha's teaching, captured birds and animals are set free, and alms are given to the poor. The celebration concludes with a candlelit procession through the streets.

Dragon Boat Festival

The Dragon Boat Festival falls on the fifth day of the fifth lunar month, usually in May or June. It commemorates the suicide in the third century BC of Qu Yuan, a respected poet and loyal and honest minister of the King of Chu, who threw himself into the Mei Lo River (in Hunan province) when the king refused to heed his advice. There are lively rowing competitions in Marina Bay between long, thin "dragon boats" to the rhythm of drums, and these are said by some people to represent attempts to rescue Qu Yuan. Special rice dumplings wrapped in bamboo leaves called *Ma Chang* are eaten, and again, these are said to have been intended for the fish (or in some versions, the dragon spirit) in the river, so that they would eat them and leave

Qu Yuan alone. Taoist ceremonies are performed on the boats before and after the races, to bless and "awaken" them beforehand and to induce them to "repose" afterward.

Hungry Ghosts Festival

The Hungry Ghosts festival takes place in the seventh Chinese lunar month, between July and August. It is thought that the restless spirits of the dead roam the earth at this time and need to be appeased with gifts of food and money. This is the most inauspicious time of the year. No marriages take place, children are discouraged from staying out late at night, and it is considered unlucky to buy property or close a deal at this time. The month is punctuated by dinners of many courses, *wayang* (Chinese street operas), auctions, and noisy celebrations to pacify the ghosts. Bonfires can be seen all over Singapore, burning offerings of replica money— and even paper cars, houses, and mobile phones—to the spirits.

National Day

The celebration of Singapore's gaining of independence on August 9 culminates in a huge parade and fireworks in the evening. All groups are represented—the ethnic communities, schoolchildren, civil organizations, and the armed forces. Each year there is a different theme, and there are weeks of practice beforehand. Tickets are even available for the dress rehearsal.

Lantern Festival

Usually falling in September, the fifteenth day of the eighth Chinese lunar month, when the moon is supposed to be brighter and fuller than at any other time of the year, this is the harvest festival of ancient China, which celebrates the legend of the moon goddess, Chang-O. Also known as the Mooncake Festival, it is celebrated by the eating of mooncakes—sweet pastries made with flour, oil, and lotus seed—and lantern displays. At night children carry brightly colored lanterns in the shape of birds and animals in a parade. A special feature of the Lantern Festival is the dragon dance, where a huge dragon head and body, supported by a team of dancers, weaves its way around the streets collecting money on its route.

Among the legends associated with mooncakes is the overthrowing of the Mongol Yuan dynasty by Chinese rebels, who sent secret messages to each other hidden in the mooncakes.

Deepavali

The Festival of Lights, Deepavali or Diwali, is celebrated at the darkest time of the year, usually in October or November, and marks the start of the New Year for Hindus. The festival celebrates the defeat of the demon Narakasura by Lord Krishna, or the triumph of light over darkness and good over evil. It is a time of rejoicing and renewal in Hindu homes. Oil lamps are lit, garlands of jasmine placed at the family altar, and family and friends visit each other. Before the festival itself, houses are cleaned and new clothes bought. This is the time for the closing of accounts, for giving gifts, and offering worship to Lakshmi, the goddess of prosperity. Throughout Little India there is a blaze of light and sound from temples, night bazaars, and performances of traditional Indian songs and dances

Hari Raya Puasa

The date of this Muslim festival varies according to the lunar calendar, and marks the end of the month-long fast of Ramadan for Malays and Indian Muslims. The holy month of Ramadan, the ninth month of the Islamic year, is observed with prayers and fasting during the hours of daylight. The celebration of the breaking of the fast begins with a tremendous housecleaning, the purchase of new clothes and, of course, the preparation of a splendid meal. Dishes include the seasonal *Ketupat*, savory rice in woven palm leaves, plus *Lontong* rice rolls in banana leaves, and the ever popular *Nasi Padang*, which means literally "rice field" and is in fact plain boiled rice served with a selection of dishes, including curry and the famous Malay *Rending*, a dry beef or chicken curry.

The celebrations last three days. The Muslims, too, give packets of money to children when they go visiting. These are usually green in color and children naturally look forward to them.

THE CHINESE LUNAR CALENDAR

Although the visitor may see the Chinese Singaporeans as very Westernized, their lives are still governed by many traditional beliefs, including ancient Chinese astrology. This can influence important life decisions such as births and marriages.

The Chinese lunar calendar is said to have been adopted in 2,698 BCE, and years are counted from then on, with some adjustments. It is a sixty-year-cycle calendar—the name of each year reappears every sixty years. Within this there are five twelve-year cycles, each year being named after one of the animals of the Chinese Zodiac, e.g., the Year of the Dog or the Year of the Monkey. Half the animals are domestic and half are wild, reflecting the

Yin-Yang balance. Within the year there are twenty-four terms that mark the changes in nature and are used by farmers as a guide for planting and harvesting.

Within the sixty-year cycle, the biggest birthday celebrations are the first and the sixtieth, when the individual starts a new life. After the sixtieth year, birthdays are celebrated every ten years. Apart from the two key birthdays, people believe that the ages of 25, 29, 33, 36, and 66 are critical, and these, too, are occasions for celebration.

BIRTHS
Chinese

The Chinese consider a baby to be one year old at birth. For the first thirty days after birth it is believed that a mother's pores remain open and that cold air can enter the body. Consequently, new Chinese mothers may be forbidden to go outdoors or take a shower or bath. Diet will be high in Yang foods, including meat, eggs, and liver, and Yin foods may be avoided. Traditionally many mothers will eat specially prepared soups and broths containing pigs' feet and chicken. The great celebration of the baby's birth takes place after this month and, as with all Chinese festivities, it centers upon food. A large number of family and friends are invited to a party, especially for a first-born child, and hard-boiled eggs with red painted shells, a universal symbol of life, are given to the guests. The guests in turn give gifts for the baby, often baby clothes in the colors of good luck—red, pink, gold, or orange, and always in matching pairs. The colors in the West that are often associated with babies, such as white or blue, are symbols of death in Singapore and are therefore taboo.

Malay

As with the Indian and Chinese communities, most Malay babies are born in hospitals today and many traditional Malay practices associated with the birth of a child have had to be abandoned. The child's name is formally bestowed on him or her forty-four days after birth, although the name will already have been registered with the civil authorities. This religious ceremony takes place at home and is often followed by a party. There is no problem about colors of gifts for the baby, and some people like to give money, discreetly enclosed in an envelope.

Indian

As with every other important aspect of life undertaken in an Indian household, a Brahmin priest draws up the baby's horoscope and this will be consulted at major events in the child's life. The great celebration of the birth itself takes place twenty-eight days after the child has come into the world, when its name is whispered into the baby's ear by the father. This is followed by a visit to the temple by mother and child to give thanks for a safe delivery and for the baby's birth hair to be shaved off. Acceptable gifts are cuddly toys and baby outfits in cheerful colors, again not white.

WEDDINGS

Chinese

Weddings are celebrated in style in Singapore. The Chinese bride dresses in the traditional white wedding dress of the West during the day, and then changes into the lucky red or pink gown for the wedding banquet in the evening. The ceremony starts with the smartly dressed groom arriving in an elaborately pink and red decorated car to collect his bride. They then proceed to the groom's house where the bride is welcomed into her new family. The couple firstly honor the household gods and pay their respects to the ancestors. The all-important tea ceremony then takes place with the bride and groom offering the groom's seated parents a cup of ceremonial tea. The father, as head of the family, sips first and then his wife. In this way the bride becomes part of and is accepted by her new family. The bride is given *Hong Bao* by her new family, which may contain either money or jewelry. At this point, all the relatives are offered tea in turn according to their position in the family. After this the younger generation receives her into the family by serving her tea. The couple then move on to the bride's house where a similar tea ceremony is performed.

The wedding banquet is usually enormous, both in terms of the number of guests and the number of courses served. The bride and groom visit every table and are toasted at each. However, some couples prefer to have a wedding buffet during the day as it is less formal, usually less expensive, and guests can dance or be entertained after the meal.

Malay

A Malay wedding is equally colorful and elaborate, and usually takes place on a Saturday evening and Sunday. On the Saturday the bride waits at her home, which has been elaborately decorated with silk and satin hangings, beaded cushions, and finely embroidered throws. She is the queen of the proceedings, while the groom and his family have to wait patiently in the hall or passageway outside. The *Berinai*, or henna application ceremony, is held prior to the wedding. The bride's palms and feet are decorated with dye from henna leaves. An official, licensed by the Muslim authorities, then speaks to the bride and groom separately, and if they agree to the marriage taking place they sign the marriage register. The groom then gives the bride a ceremonial wedding gift of about $100 and they salaam each other. The couple are then legally married, but they do not start living together until after the *Bersanding*, or the sitting in state ceremony, the next day.

The *Bersanding* is the public celebration of the wedding and is held at the bride's home. In modern Singapore this usually means the landscaped area at the entrance to the HDB estate or in the enormous elevator lobby of the block where the girl lives. Marquees for the guests and a sumptuously decorated raised platform for the thrones for the bride and groom are hired. The couple reign as King and Queen over their guests and the guests sprinkle rose petals and then saffron rice on their palms. This ritual is to wish the happy couple a fruitful life together. In return the guests are given chocolate or a cake in a glass, symbolizing and celebrating fertility for the marriage. During this time the bride is supposed to sit with her eyes downcast and not to smile, in order to show modesty and decorum. Finally, after the bride and groom step down from their thrones a traditional banquet is served.

Some couples today like to have a Western-style reception as well, usually in a hotel, for their work colleagues. For this the bride will be dressed in a Western-style wedding dress.

Indian

The Hindu wedding ceremony traditionally takes hours, but some couples opt for a much simpler ceremony. The important part is when the bride and groom, watched by the priest, walk around the sacred fire that represents purity, followed by the groom's tying of the *thali*, a gold chain, around his bride's neck. The *thali* is the equivalent of the Western wedding ring, and this part of the ceremony is very noisy, with the ringing of bells and shouts and chants in order to keep evil spirits at bay. Elaborately dressed guests, in saris and adorned with gold jewelry, then throw yellow rice on the newly married couple and give them gifts of either money or jewelry. Even when Indian Christians marry in church, the tying of the *thali* around the bride's neck is an important part of the ceremony.

FUNERALS
Chinese

Chinese funerals are highly organized and ritualistic affairs, and the ceremonies can continue for up to seven days until the body is cremated. The first ceremony takes place just after death, when the chief mourner washes the deceased. If the death has occurred in one of the high-rise apartment blocks, the body is taken down by way of the stairs and the embalming and the placing in the coffin is carried out in the open area beneath the apartment block. This is where the mourners gather; sometimes wealthy families hire extra mourners. Food and drink are provided and the mourners sit around and play mah-jong. Loud music is played to keep away evil spirits and also animals, if the gathering is outside.

If in doubt, foreigners should check with colleagues as to whether it is appropriate to attend the wake. The etiquette at the wake involves filing past the open coffin. You then pay your respects to the bereaved. At this stage Singaporeans generally make a small gift to help with the funeral expenses.

On the day of the funeral the mourners assemble and set off in a cavalcade led by a brightly colored van with the symbol of the tiger, if the person was a male, and the stork, if it was a woman. In China the tiger is lord of the animals. It is the emblem of might and courage, and the white tiger is the guardian of graves. The stork is not only a messenger of the gods, who can carry a person to heaven, but also a symbol of virtue. The procession usually consists of family mourners followed by colorfully dressed musicians. The priest and the hearse follow behind. The bereaved wear sackcloth headbands and straw sandals. The body is normally cremated, in contrast to the Chinese mainland tradition, reflecting the realities of population density. After the funeral the important ritual of providing the deceased with all the material goods needed in the next life takes place. Traditionally these items were buried with the body, but today houses, cars, and mobile phones made of paper are ceremonially burned, after which the funeral party shares a large meal.

Muslim

When a Muslim dies the Imam is summoned to the house. The body is placed with the head facing Mecca, and washed by relatives, after which a white cloth is placed over it. It is the tradition in Islam for the deceased to be buried within twelve hours of death; until then someone stays with the body with the Imam reciting prayers. Finally the body is wrapped in more layers of cloth, the last being seamless, and is then taken either to the mosque or directly to the graveyard.

Indian

In the Indian community, when the deceased is a Hindu, the body, after washing, is placed in a wooden coffin with silver coins on the eyes to keep them closed. Two oil lamps are set on either side of the coffin, and the grandchildren process around with lighted candles. The funeral rite is conducted in the home, followed immediately by cremation. As a mark of respect for the dead person, an oil lamp remains burning in the home for as long as forty days after death.

GIFT GIVING

Generally speaking, gifts are given at weddings, Christmas, and Chinese New Year. The main point to remember for all three ethnic groups is that the

present should be suitable for the occasion. It
would be better not to give a gift at all than to give
something cheap and tawdry. Don't
hand out promotional
ballpoint pens or keyrings to
negotiating partners!
Furthermore, presents
should always be wrapped.
It would be considered
impolite to present an unwrapped
gift with the words "I'm sorry I didn't have time to
wrap it." For in Singapore it is not only the thought
that counts, but also how the thought is presented.
An unwrapped present demonstrates your view of
the recipient—he or she is not important enough
for the gift to be wrapped.

It is worth remembering, not only for
Singapore but also for the rest of Asia, that form is
of the essence. It is not just what you do that is
important, but how you do it.

Chinese

The Chinese have many superstitions and you
soon learn in Singapore that certain colors,
numbers, and everyday items have propitious or
other connotations. Buildings and interiors
should be designed according to the principles of
Feng Shui, for example, having no sharp edges to
ensure harmony.

Red, gold, and pink are the colors associated with good luck and health, fortune and happiness, while white, blue, navy blue, and black are associated with mourning. So the "Little Black Dress" is not a favorite item in a traditional Chinese woman's wardrobe, nor the white linen suit associated with life in the tropics for a man.

Similarly, even numbers are looked upon favorably as everything is in a pair and harmonious, while an uneven number signifies loneliness and imbalance. The exceptions to this are 4, 14, and 24, which are unlucky to many Chinese because in Cantonese the number four sounds like the word "dead."

With the exception of Valentine's Day bouquets (no doubt the traditional red roses symbolize harmony, love, and good fortune), flowers are not given by the Chinese in Singapore, as they are associated with illness and death. Do not, therefore, send flowers to a new mother; and do not send a card with a stork on it, as a symbolic stork adorns a woman's funeral procession.

A gift of a clock—a favorite retirement gift in the West—would be most inappropriate, as the word "clock" in Cantonese also sounds like "go to a funeral"! Other items to be avoided include handkerchiefs, as they are dispensed at funerals, and sharp objects, like scissors or penknives, which signify the end of a friendship.

When the Chinese give gifts, on occasions such
as Chinese New Year or at weddings, they like to
give *Hong Bao*—money, preferably brand-new
notes, in a red envelope. If you are invited to a
wedding and do not know how much to give, ask
local advice. This will not be seen as a *faux pas* on
your part, but shows that you are sensitive to
another culture and want to do, and especially be
seen to do, the right thing.

In Singapore, as elsewhere in Asia, it is not the
custom to unwrap a gift in front of the giver, but
simply to accept it with great pleasure. In this way
no embarrassment is felt by either the giver or the
receiver when the gift is finally unwrapped.

Malay

When giving gifts to Malays, always remember
that they are Muslims—although a Chinese
colleague would be delighted with a gift of
brandy, a Malay would be horrified. Similarly, do
not give perfume to a woman if it contains
alcohol, and do not give gifts made from pigskin.
If attending a wedding, a nice present would be

something for the kitchen, such as a tea set, kitchen utensils (but again, not knives), serving dishes, saucepans, and so on. The present can be wrapped in traditional wedding paper or red (for love) paper. Unlike the Chinese, people do not usually give money at Malay weddings.

Gifts are not usually given to a new mother, but if you wish to do so, a basket of fruit is always appreciated. When visiting the mother and newborn baby at home it is traditional to bring a gift for the baby: clothing or cuddly toys, but remember—no dogs!

Indian

Like the Chinese and Malays, the Indians do not open presents in front of the giver. Unlike the Malays, the Indians believe that it is good luck to give a sum of money, if appropriate (such as for a wedding), in odd numbers, and this is often done by adding one dollar to a multiple of ten dollars, for example fifty-one dollars.

When an Indian baby is born, a gift of gold, such as a bracelet, is often given. Baby clothes and soft toys—again, no dogs if the family is Muslim—are also appropriate.

Although frangipani is considered beautiful and exotic by Western visitors, do not give it as a present to Indians or decorate your home or hotel room with it. It is the flower used in funeral wreaths by the Indian community. Also avoid beef products or anything made of leather when giving a gift to Hindus. If giving money to a Tamil, the opposite rule to the Chinese applies: the notes must be given in odd numbers. If you are at all worried by this, simply seek local advice when giving a gift.

chapter four

THE SINGAPOREANS AT HOME

SOCIAL AND FAMILY RELATIONSHIPS

Although it is now rare to find all three
generations living under the same roof, as would
have been the case in China, India, or Malaysia,
the belief in the extended family is still strong. For
all three ethnic groups, the most important social
unit in society is the family, and that means the
extended family. It is the means by which
traditional values are passed on to the next
generation so that one's precious cultural identity
in this land of immigrants will not be lost. It is
from the family that religious practice is learned,
and it is from the family that the child learns to be
a good Singaporean citizen. Consequently, no
important decision is made without the family's
approval, whether it concerns the choice of school
or university, a likely marriage partner, or
business or employment decisions. Young men
and women do not form attachments and date if
their parents do not approve of the potential
girlfriend or boyfriend, and this possibly goes
some way to explain why there are so few

interracial marriages. When there is an interracial marriage, the children take the father's ethnicity.

Singapore is still largely a patriarchal society, although from its inception the government has been determined that men and women should be equal before the law and should have equal opportunities in education and employment.

CHILDREN

The public displays of affection that are frowned on in Singapore do not apply to babies and young children. Indeed, it is true to say that they are overwhelmed by love, and often, to Western eyes, overindulged, for a preschooler can do no wrong. The thinking behind this is that the real world, with all its triumphs and disappointments, does not begin until a child starts school.

Great value is placed on education, not only by the parents, who see it as improving the quality of their child's future, but also by the state, which sees it as the necessary lifeblood of the nation. A student is therefore expected to work hard at school and spend long hours doing homework. All three groups learn not only their own ethnic language but also English, and they are expected to be fluent in both. In the early years after independence many Chinese parents could not understand the reasoning behind this and argued that under British rule their children were allowed to be educated completely in Chinese, yet under their own elected government they also had to learn English. Nobody now doubts the wisdom of Lee Kuan Yew's insistence on English being taught in all schools, for not only has it been a conduit to economic success, but it serves as a common language in a country that did not have one.

LIFESTYLE AND HOUSING

The really wealthy live in palatial houses on "landed property." Affluent Singaporeans live in large, luxurious private apartments complete with swimming pools and squash courts. They are very much in the minority. About 85 percent of all families live in high-rise HDB apartments that they are either buying or aiming to buy. The apartments are well furnished and contain all the latest electronic and technical gadgets.

INVITATIONS HOME

Gifts

It is always appreciated if the visitor brings a gift, but remember the Malays and Indian Muslims do not drink alcohol and frown upon smoking, so sweets or cakes are a good idea. If your hosts are Chinese, remember to keep to even numbers, except 4, 14, and 24, which are unlucky.

Etiquette

It is a great and rare privilege to be invited to a Singaporean home, and so as not to give offense here are some points to be aware of. In all three communities it is the custom to remove your shoes when entering the home (so wear socks or tights). Remember to dress modestly. It is probably better to dress more formally than you might normally dress if visiting Western friends— so no shorts or revealing clothes, even if it is hot and humid outside.

In Malay homes you may well be invited to sit on the floor, and here you have to be careful not to point the soles of your feet at anyone, so if you are a man sit cross legged and if you are a woman, sitting sideways with your feet tucked under you usually solves the problem.

If, however, you are invited to sit on a sofa or a chair, it is a good idea not to cross your legs, especially in front of an older person, as this is regarded as rude. Where children are concerned, in the West it is usual to pat a small child or toddler on the head, but in the Malay and Indian world the head is considered to be sacred and should never be touched. Above all, do not use the left hand when eating, shaking hands, or giving gifts in Malay or Indian households, as it is reserved for personal hygiene and considered unclean.

In all three communities it is the tradition to offer some refreshment, however brief the visit, and it would be impolite to refuse. If you are invited to a meal in the evening, remember that Singaporeans tend to rise early and retire early, so take your cue from your hosts. Unlike in the West, guests may not stay on after the meal but leave promptly when it is finished.

Public and Private Areas

Singaporeans have definite public and private areas, and the visitor can cause grave embarrassment if in conversation he unwittingly touches on close personal or family relationships, emotions, romantic attachments, or sexual matters. Displays of affection are frowned upon and the Western habit of hugging and kissing close personal friends of the opposite sex is not even considered. Similarly, discussions about religion or the political environment are best avoided, and humor does not always travel well—especially British humor, which is often self-deprecating.

GREETINGS

Chinese people will often shake hands, but it is not the firm, vigorous grip of North America or Northern Europe, but rather a softer more gentle gesture. You will also probably see an older Chinese man pat a younger friend on the arm as a way of greeting.

When greeting each other, Malays will probably salaam, that is, put their palms together and make a small bow. They might use the other traditional Malay greeting of offering both hands to the recipient, lightly touching the person's outstretched hands, then bringing one or two hands back to the heart. Your hosts, knowing you are Western and wanting you to feel at home, may very well shake your hand, but again, Malay women do not expect to shake hands with a man and a Malay man would not generally expect to shake hands with a Western woman. Unlike countries in continental Europe and South America, Singaporeans do not go in for hugging or kissing, even with close friends.

Similarly, in the Indian community different sexes do not shake hands with one another, although an Indian woman will shake hands with another woman and a man with another man. The traditional Indian greeting of *namaste* is similar to that of the Malay salaam.

PUBLIC DISPLAY

All the communities respect age because of the wisdom it brings and expect dignified behavior in front of an older person. They all feel uncomfortable with public displays of affection, and with touching members of the opposite sex, so a handshake may not be an appropriate greeting. It is a good idea to maintain a reasonable social distance, about an arm's length, away from the opposite sex. This is slightly further away than most Westerners are familiar with. A friendly smile and nod of acknowledgment gets around any difficulty. In contrast, Singaporeans of the same sex touch freely and hold hands as signs of friendship and closeness, nothing more.

BOY MEETS GIRL

Interracial marriages are rare as cultural influences are so strong. Dating and courtship within the three communities of Singapore is a relatively new phenomenon. Marriage was considered far too important a matter to be left to casual dating and romance—it was seen as the final step into adult life and responsibility, necessary for the creation of the next generation. Romantic love was considered a bonus in marriage and not obligatory, and most marriages were arranged by parents who considered that they knew and understood their children better than they did themselves. The parents would try to find a partner from a similar background, whose personality would be compatible, thereby ensuring as far as possible that the marriage would be harmonious.

In the past, and on occasion even now, especially if the young person is shy and reserved, Singaporean families would use a matchmaker to find the ideal partner for their child. In this way they would ensure that religious, social, and educational criteria were properly considered, and, in the case of an Indian betrothal, that caste laws were strictly adhered to. Horoscopes for both Chinese and Indian families would be studied carefully, as would the background of the prospective bride or groom, and if anything untoward were found, the marriage would definitely not go ahead.

Today young people in all three communities are encouraged to get to know each other as friends and to have a social life of dinners, outings, and parties as part of a group. In conservative Singaporean families, individual dating as known in the West, where a boy or girl has many dates, is frowned upon, and indeed this kind of behavior could jeopardize their marriage prospects. So young people get to know each other at school, university, and in the various social clubs attached to their places of employment.

Dating below the age of seventeen is also disapproved of, as parents feel their children should spend their time on their all-important studies and preserve their good reputations. Thereafter, when a boy and girl decide that they like each other, and more importantly if the parents approve of the prospective partner, they will start going out together as a couple. This is usually the precursor to marriage, and so it is important that a Western visitor realizes exactly what dating means in Singapore. If by any chance the boy or girl's family feels unhappy with the dating arrangements, then the young people will take note of their wishes not to proceed. In the Indian community dating does not start until after the engagement has taken place.

NATIONAL SERVICE

At the age of sixteen and a half, every Singaporean
male has to do two to two-and-a-half years'
national service, and later reserve duty until the
age of forty. This is a useful opportunity for the
different strands of society to mix and work
together. The experience of being thrown together
with people from different backgrounds for a
common purpose creates social ties and fosters a
shared sense of identity. Position and promotion
in the army depends on performance. The
government may choose to defer national service
for target groups to suit the social and economic
needs of the moment, but no one is exempt.

NAMES

In Singapore the three ethnic groups refer to
themselves in very different ways and because this
is still a formal society it is important to get
personal names and titles correct. If ever in doubt,
seek local advice for it will show that you are
sensitive to the issue.

The correct forms of address in Singapore can
be complicated. Generally, when making
introductions and in formal meetings it is
advisable to use a person's title first and then their
family or personal name, for example "Vice
President Lee." Titles are usually used for

superiors, but not for equals or juniors. Although many younger Singaporeans adopt a Western-style personal name, such as Lucy or Brian Wong, for everyday use, most elder Singaporeans do not, and it is always better to err on the side of formality rather than give offense.

Chinese

Chinese conventions can be fraught with difficulty for the Western visitor, and something of a revelation when you work out the system.

Given the importance of family to the Chinese, it comes as no surprise that the family name is given precedence in the order of an individual's names. For example, if a man's family name is Wong he would be called "Mr. Wong." Mr. Wong probably has two given names, so he might be Wong Chok Yew. This is where it gets slightly complicated, because the name Chok will have been given to all the sons of that generation in the family. Finally, he will have his personal name, Yew. Therefore Mr. Wong's full name is presented, from the general to the particular, as Wong Chok Yew.

When being formal it is a good idea to address somebody as Mr., Miss, or Madam, followed by the family name, for example "Miss Lee." Friends call each other by their given names. In business, take your cue from your counterpart.

Chinese women, on the other hand,

traditionally retain their own (paternal) family name on marriage as they are obviously not of the bloodline of the husband. So Mr. Wong's wife is technically not Mrs. Wong, although she might be known by her Western friends by this name. If her maiden name was Lee Bee Wah, in which Lee was the paternal family name, it remained the same when she married and she became Mrs Lee. Sometimes Chinese women changed their name by joining it with that of their husband—in this case she would have been Mrs. Lee-Wong Bee Wah. Occasionally the honorific title of Madam was used, as in Madam Mao Tse Tung or Madam Chang Kai Shek.

In Singapore, Chinese women tend to use their husband's name. If they want to retain their own name, they use their maiden name plus "Madam."

Chinese women, like the men, will often adopt a Western personal name, especially if working for a foreign company, so Lee Bee Wah might refer to herself as "Betty."

If all this seems a little too complicated, just ask people what they would like to be called. And remember, Chinese people are equally bemused by Western names, especially if a person's name is Robert and suddenly they hear him being referred to as Bob, or Alexandra as Sandra. Tell your Chinese friends and colleagues what you want to be called from the beginning so that you avoid the embarrassing situation of being referred to in the office as Mr. Robert or Miss Alexandra.

In Singapore, children refer to older people who are not related—parents' friends, shopkeepers, salesmen, hawkers—as "Auntie" or "Uncle." Foreigners are sometimes bemused to hear the term used in unlikely circumstances.

Malay

Malay men attach their father's name to the end of their own name and use the word *bin*, which means "son of." So, for example, Ali bin Osman is Ali, son of Osman.

Similarly women use *binti*, or "daughter of." So Fatima binti Osman is Fatima, daughter of Osman. Her friends will call her Fatima and in more formal terms she will be addressed as *Puan* (Mrs.) Fatima or Mrs. Fatima. As with the Chinese and Indian communities, some Malay married women (especially those in business) will adopt their husband's name in the Western manner. If you see the word *Hajji* or the feminine *Hajjiah* in a person's name, it means that he or she has undertaken the pilgrimage to Mecca.

Indian

The forebears of the majority of the Indians in Singapore came from Tamil Nadu, where they do not use family names. Instead they use the initial of their father's name placed before their own personal name. For example, a woman named Radhika would call herself M. Radhika, where M is the first letter of the name of her father, Murugesan. After marriage, Radhika will be addressed as Mrs. Radhika, followed by her husband's personal name or both his names.

Not all Indians in Singapore are Hindu or Muslim—some are Sikh and others Christian. Unlike the Chinese, if you hear an Indian refer to himself by his Christian name, such as Thomas or Patrick, then he will indeed be a Christian, and this is not just a Western name he has adopted for ease of pronunciation.

Most Sikhs have three names: a personal name, a name to show Sikh identity ("Singh," or "lion" for a male), and a clan or sub-sect name. Many Sikh names are the same as, or similar to, Hindu ones. All Sikhs are Singhs, but not all Singhs are Sikhs. (Singh, meaning lion, is included in the name of Singapore!) Men are often addressed as "Sardarji" (abbreviated to S.), which is an honorific similar to "Mr." Most personal names can be used for both males and females. Women often just use "Kaur" (meaning "princess") as a third name, but can also use "Singh," as many families have taken this as a surname.

chapter five

FOOD & DRINK

Food plays an important role in the social life of Singaporeans. The blending and adapting of the Chinese, Malay, and Indian culinary traditions has resulted in a distinctive new cuisine. Typical Singapore dishes range from the classic Chili Crab, Hokkien Prawn Noodle soup, and *Murtabak* (stuffed Indian bread), to more recent introductions such as Stingray in Banana Leaf (from Malaysia), and tea-smoked Sea Bass. Smoking food over a mixture of tea leaves is popular in Yunnan and Sichuan provinces of China, but there it is usually done with duck.

The fusion of these strong traditions began in Singapore's earliest days. Indeed, it could be said that the modern fashionable idea of "fusion food" first started in Singapore.

Due to the huge influx of Chinese migrants, Malay food soon incorporated such Chinese staples as bean sprouts, soy sauce, noodles, and bean curd. Spicy *Kangkung* is a good example of a dish where both Malay and Chinese seasonings are used to bring out the flavor of the leafy green vegetable *kangkung*. Straits Chinese from Malaysia combine Nonya cuisine with the Chinese love of pork, which, of course, is forbidden to Malay Muslims. Similarly, Chinese noodles are often served in a spicy coconut broth, as in *Mee Siam*. Again, this is a firm favorite in Nonya cuisine, but not seen in mainland China.

If Chili Crab is Singapore's national dish, Fish Head Curry is not far behind. This was a recipe invented fifty years ago by a young chef, originally from Kerala. This dish is not seen in his native South India, but to the Chinese the head of the fish, and especially the cheek pocket, is the most succulent and delicate part. Matched with a curry sauce, it soon became a firm favorite and today there are many variations and interpretations of this curry.

The local Indian population has also produced an Indian variation of Indonesian *Mee Goreng*— fried wheat noodles with chilies, potato, and bean sprouts—served with a spicy curry sauce. One way in which the Chinese will eat mutton is in the hearty North Indian Mutton Soup. It is always a popular dish in the food stands as it makes a great lunch or late night supper dish. The soup is enlivened with lots of fresh coriander as well as other dried spices and, to give it a new twist, it is served with crunchy French bread. *Murtabak*, a classic Indian Muslim dish consisting of bread stuffed with minced meat and onion, is very popular.

Chilies, which are essential in Indian cooking but not in Chinese, apart from the northern provinces of Sichuan and Hunan, appear in nearly every Singaporean Chinese noodle or rice dish. Indeed, it would be hard to imagine these dishes without them.

More surprising, though, is the fact that Singaporeans have also been influenced by the food of their former colonial masters. Fruit chutneys, tomato ketchup, Worcestershire sauce, and more recently balsamic vinegar, have all been a source of inspiration, as well as potatoes and slow-oven baking. A vaguely English oxtail stew was often cooked by Hainanese cooks in colonial homes, and this has now been interpreted in a Malay/Indonesian style as Sour Hot Oxtail Stew, or *Buntut Asam Pedas*.

Indonesian cuisine is represented in the widespread use of fragrant spices such as galangal, a root similar in appearance to ginger. As the ancestors of many Malay Singaporeans came from Java, a firm favorite is the Javanese Spicy Chicken Soup with Noodles, or *Soto Ayam*. Braised Fish in Pickled Vegetables, or *Acar Ikan*, is another traditional Malay/Indonesian dish. Satays are also very popular but, unlike in Indonesian and Malaysian cuisine, in Singapore they have been adapted to Chinese tastes, and are therefore often made with pork.

COOKING STYLES

Barbecuing and grilling, long used by cooks in Malaysia, soon joined Chinese stir-frying, braising, and steaming techniques. Different provinces of China—depending on the climate and cooking fuel available—developed different culinary styles, and it is true to say that all of these are in use in Singapore. Although the Cantonese community is relatively small, this is not reflected in the many Cantonese restaurants and in the widespread enjoyment of *Dim Sum*, a popular Hong Kong lunchtime dish. Hokkien food is strong on pork, which Indian and Malay Muslims are forbidden to eat, but the Hokkien *mee*—the yellow wheat noodles—are popular with everyone. Indeed, they have been incorporated into Malay dishes such as *Mee Rebus* or *Soto Mee* and the Indian/Indonesian *Mee Goreng*.

Teochew food relies heavily on fish. Indeed, the men of Teochew in Southern China were traditionally fishermen. The Teochew fish ball, like the Hokkien *mee*, is accepted by all creeds. In fact the Chinese, being the good businesspeople they are, have gone further than this and established *Halal* (food prepared according to Muslim dietary laws) Chinese restaurants where their Muslim neighbors can comfortably eat, safe in the knowledge that they are not breaking any of their food laws.

DIETARY RESTRICTIONS

The Chinese, apart from Buddhists in the South of China who do not eat beef, have no restrictions on what they can or cannot eat—perhaps because of a history of years of famine and desperate poverty, everything is fair game. Indeed, the Chinese greeting is not "Hello" or "How are you?" but "Have you eaten?" The reply, incidentally, is always "Yes," even if you haven't.

However, that does not mean to say that all Singaporean Chinese like the same food: mutton and lamb are highly prized in the north of China but heartily disliked everywhere else, largely because of the smell, and this applies to the Singaporeans who come from South China. Dark chicken meat to the Chinese is the delicacy, not the white. In general they dislike large slabs of meat, and especially underdone meat such as rare steak. In China people from the north like noodles, steamed bread, and dumplings because the climate is too severe to grow rice; whereas rice is popular in the more wet and humid south. In Singapore both rice and noodles are popular.

Although the Chinese love to eat, they eat with health very much in mind. They believe that certain foods are "Yin," or "cooling." Foods such as pork, watermelon, and apples cool the body down and are good in summer. "Yang" foods on the other hand are considered to be hearty: fried foods, chocolate, and lychees are examples that fit into this category. You are guaranteed a healthy diet by balancing Yin and Yang foods. In other words: everything in moderation.

Malay and Indian Muslims are forbidden certain foods, with pork being at the top of the list. All other meats and poultry have to be slaughtered according to strict *Halal* rules.

FOOD COURTS

Hawkers once roamed the streets of Singapore selling all kinds of tasty foods. Now they have been relocated to permanent centers, but the tasty snacks have not changed.

These open-air hawker centers are not for quiet, elegant dining. They are bustling, noisy places, full of smells coming from steaming pots and sizzling pans, with orders being frequently

shouted to the cooks. Many Singaporeans
regularly eat out at such venues and all have their
favorite places. They represent excellent value for
the money and there are those who swear that the
meals in such places are just as good as, if not
better than, meals served in many upscale
restaurants. Certainly these are the places to enjoy
the best *Mee Goreng*, *Wan Tan Mee* (noodles
served with stuffed dumplings), and *Char Kway
Tiao* (stir-fried rice noodles).

In the shopping malls, air-conditioned food
courts serve hawker food, but in greater comfort.

DRINK

Chinese tea is the normal accompaniment to a
meal. The Chinese believe that it prevents obesity
by washing away the fats ingested with the food,
and when taken after a meal it helps digestion.
They do not drink coffee after meals.
Furthermore, they like to drink one or two glasses
of Chinese tea before a banquet, where there are
going to be many alcoholic toasts.

As a general rule, the Chinese do not like
drinking without eating and therefore dislike
cocktail parties. They will drink beer with their
meal, usually the splendid local Singapore brew
"Tiger Beer," and, surprisingly, given their dislike
of iced drinks, they drink it cold. They also like

drinking brandy—the more expensive the better, as it is seen as a status symbol. For Indian and Malay Muslims alcohol is strictly forbidden.

This section would not be complete without mentioning the legendary Long Bar of the Raffles Hotel, source of Singapore's most celebrated cocktail, the Singapore Sling.

SINGAPORE SLING

Original Recipe
2 parts Gin
1 part Cherry Brandy
1 part Benedictine
1 part Triple Sec
2 parts Pineapple Juice
2 parts Orange Juice
1 part Lime Juice

Quick and Simple Recipe
3 parts Gin
1 part Cherry Brandy
Juice of 1 Lemon

In both recipes mix and strain into a tall glass, top
with soda water, and decorate with sliced orange,
lemon or lime, and a cherry.

chapter six

TIME OUT

TOURISM

Singapore, given the convenience of its Changi airport hub and the pains of jet lag for the intercontinental traveler, has set out to attract the stopover visitor. It actively promotes the comfort of a few days in one of its luxurious hotels, with the opportunity to taste its appealing mix of cultures in the dramatic modern city, or to unwind and enjoy the peace of a timeless backwater idyll.

Shopping in a tax-free city flowing with international fashion designer labels gives the satisfying sense of getting a bargain that appeals to shoppers, however many dollars they have in their pockets.

Tourism contributes about 5 percent to Singapore's GDP and is strongly promoted by the government. The reputation for being a safe destination with superb hotels continues to attract millions of visitors each year. However, in 2003 the number fell from around 7.5 million per annum of the last few years to just over 6 million, almost all due to the SARS virus that reduced travel to most Asian countries. Nevertheless Singapore continues to receive regional awards for tourism, whether for the private individual, the businessman, or the convention visitor.

GETTING AROUND

Transportation in and around Singapore, whether by taxi, bus, or Mass Rapid Transit (MRT), is easy and relatively cheap. A good way to see the sights and get an idea of the geography is to take a guided cruise of the Singapore River with a commentary.

MRT

The MRT is one of the most efficient underground rail networks in the world. Trains run everyday from 5:30 a.m. until midnight. They are clean, air-conditioned, and, best of all, outside the city center of Singapore the tracks run overground. Remember to keep some small change not only for the MRT ticket but also for the buses. A souvenir card with a stored value of $5.50 in fares is available for $6.00, the $0.50 being a premium as you keep the ticket as a souvenir.

Buses and Trams

The bus network is far more comprehensive than the MRT, and slightly cheaper. Buses are also air-conditioned and operate daily from 6:00 a.m. until midnight. There is a tourist bus that covers most of the sights and runs daily from 9:00 a.m. to 6:00 p.m. Another good way to sightsee is to take a tram called the Singapore Trolley, which travels along the Orchard Road, the old colonial area, the Singapore River, and passes Raffles Hotel. You can purchase a ticket either from your hotel or the driver and this will entitle you to unlimited journeys and a riverboat tour.

Taxis

Taxis are plentiful on the streets of Singapore and you can hail them or pick them up at designated stands. Fares are reasonable, and every taxi has them clearly displayed. All cabs are metered and tipping is not expected. Remember though that if you are traveling in the city center—known as the Restricted Zone—you will have to pay a congestion charge; there is a surcharge at peak period times, and also after midnight.

Singaporean taxi drivers may not always speak English very well, and it is worth having your destination written down in English.

Trains

Regular train services run between Singapore and
key cities and towns on the west coast of Malaysia.
For a really luxurious trip, try the Eastern and
Oriental Express. It departs from Tanjong Pagar
Railway Station and takes in the sights of Penang
and the River Kwai.

Rickshaws

In Singapore you can also hire a rickshaw, or
"trishaw" as it is known locally. This is a three-
wheeled bicycle with a carriage on the back. Today
these are only a tourist attraction, not a regular
form of transportation. Remember to negotiate
the price before you commence your journey.

Car Rental

On the other hand, there is no negotiating the cost
of renting a car. Rentals are high, parking is
expensive, and the government has introduced
disincentives in order to combat traffic congestion.
The only benefit of a car would be if you were
planning to continue your trip into Malaysia.

Driving is on the left and, of course, if you
drive into the Restricted Zone in the center of the
city there is a charge to pay. The speed limit is 30
miles (50 km) an hour, and 50 miles (80 km) on
an expressway. Driving under the influence of
drugs or alcohol is dealt with severely.

DESTINATIONS
Chinatown

The first Chinese immigrants, who arrived in 1819, were allocated an area south of the Singapore River to settle in by Sir Stamford Raffles. Soon thousands of others arrived, largely from the central and southern Chinese coastal provinces, and Chinatown became a lively trading settlement. This it remained until the 1970s, when the government started to replace the old buildings with modern HDB apartments. Belatedly it was realized that this threatened the loss of yet another atmospheric part of old Singapore, and the city architects began a program of renovation and restoration, so that some of the old shops selling paper goods to burn at funerals, teas and teapots, red paper lanterns, Chinese books, and traditional clothing have been retained.

Here you get a feeling of what Singapore must have been like in the early 1900s—bustling streets, noisy with the sound of different dialects, filled with the pungent scents of food cooking, and thronged with people. Many of the shop houses were two or three stories high, depending on the family's affluence. Sadly some have had to be demolished in recent years due to the construction of the MRT that has led to new stations at Clarke

Quay and Chinatown, but at least this makes it easy for the traveler to visit the area.

The best way to explore Chinatown is on foot, giving yourself at least three or four hours. Not only is there a lot to see, but the weather is hot and humid and can be debilitating if you are not used to it. Take along plenty of sunscreen and a good pair of sunglasses, and wear a broad-brimmed hat.

Arab Street

The area north of the Singapore River and west of the Rochor River was designated a Muslim settlement by Raffles and soon attracted Arab traders. Today it still reflects the traditions of those Arab seafarers, Indonesians, and Malays who came to settle here. The shops of Arab Street are a blaze of color, selling cloth of all kinds, including silks and batik, rugs, brassware, gold, and jewelry, as well as rattan ware and basketry that overflow onto the sidewalk. The air is filled with the marvelous smells coming from the many Halal restaurants, especially around the Sultan Mosque.

The first mosque was built on the island in 1826 thanks to a generous grant from the East India Company. One hundred years later, the Islamic community had outgrown this and the Sultan Mosque was built. This is now the city's principal mosque. It can accommodate five thousand worshipers and has a golden dome,

towers, and minarets. Visits are strictly regulated and the best time to come is during the month of Ramadan—when the sun sets and Muslims can break their fast, the surrounding streets are full of enticing food stands.

The name Arab Street applies not only to the street itself but to the whole area bounded by Rochor Canal Road, Jalan Sultan, Victoria Street, and Beach Road. The easiest way to get there is to take the MRT to Bugis.

Little India

Little India, surprisingly considering the history of Chinatown and Arab Street, was not designated as an ethnic quarter, but simply grew of its own volition in the latter half of the nineteenth century. It is largely concentrated north of the Rochor Canal and is easy to get to—simply take the MRT and alight at Little India station. The main artery, Seragoon Road, stretches a mile from Rochor Canal Road to Lavender Street, and can easily be explored on foot. Brace yourself for a sensory experience—there is so much to see, delicious foods to smell and sample, and wonderful items to buy.

There are goldsmiths selling jewelry created from ancient Indian patterns. The Little India Arcade, a cluster of shops from the colonial era, sells sari fabrics—some with gold and silver threads woven into them. Visitors sometimes buy lengths of sari material for use as exotic bed hangings back home, or as elaborate table runners. The nearby "Spice Route" shop is worth visiting to see or, perhaps more importantly, to smell the ground mixed spices. The brightly packaged spices make unusual gifts, and they come with the added bonus of easy-to-make recipes.

All this can easily take a good half day, and Sundays are best avoided unless you like crowds. Sunday is the day when migrant workers from all over South Asia come here to chat, eat, worship, and shop, and at times it can seem as if the entire subcontinent has gathered here!

Historic Singapore

At the heart of the old colonial settlement is the Padang ("field" in Malay), a large, well-tended open space surrounded by trees that was earmarked by Raffles as a recreation ground soon after his arrival. Here are the grand colonial buildings that are still used for the city's administration. Many were designed by the Irish architect George Coleman, and if you later wander up to the first fort on the island, Fort Canning, you can see his gravestone together with those of other early settlers. It is a sobering exercise to read the inscriptions on these headstones as so many of the first British arrivals died in their twenties, killed not by war but by tropical diseases. The hill itself, in addition to containing the ruins of the fort, is landscaped with shrubs and trees.

Raffles Hotel

A visit to Singapore would not be complete without a visit to the legendary Raffles Hotel.

Since opening its doors in 1887 it has epitomized colonial elegance, luxury, and style, and given rise to an exotic cocktail—the Singapore Sling (see page 105). Writers such as Joseph Conrad, Rudyard Kipling, and Somerset Maugham stayed here, as did glamorous Hollywood movie stars like Ava Gardner and Elizabeth Taylor.

Chinese Garden

For those interested in gardening or in search of a few peaceful hours' relaxation, a trip to the Chinese Garden and the nearby Japanese Garden, at any time other than the weekend, is very worthwhile. Both are close to the MRT Chinese Garden station to the west of the city.

Sentosa

This tiny island, immediately south of Singapore, was formerly a British military base. It is now a favorite resort for locals and tourists alike. One of the main attractions is the Underwater World, the largest oceanarium in Asia. A moving walkway through two huge tanks allows you to view exotic fish such as giant rays and thick-lipped garoupa close up. If your visit coincides with one of the many feeding times, it can be even more exciting. It is a good idea to check the times beforehand.

The colorful Butterfly Park with some 2,500 specimens is also worth visiting, and of course, this being Singapore, there are the beautiful but inevitable orchid gardens.

If you fancy being a little less active, a visit to the southwestern coast of the island will take you to sparkling beaches created from specially imported sand, coconut palms, and flowering shrubs.

The Smaller St. John's and Pulau Ubin Islands
For the more adventurous, there is also St. John's Island, just under four miles (six km) south of Singapore, which is less developed than Sentosa. There are no hotels there, but there are some magnificent former colonial bungalows to rent. You can swim in the lagoons, picnic in certain designated spots, and watch a wide variety of bird life, some of which has made a successful bid for freedom from the bird sellers on the main island. It takes about an hour to get to St. John's and the ferries leave from the World Trade Center. Check with your hotel for the times of sailings.

If you really want to step back in time to see the Singapore of fifty years ago, visit the island of Pulau Ubin, about one and a half miles (two km) off the northeastern corner of Singapore. You can simply sit looking out to sea, admire the traditional Malay stilt fishing huts, or visit one of the Taoist or Buddhist temples on the island. The more energetic can rent mountain bikes to explore the forests and the mangrove swamps that abound with wildlife. Details of these activities can be obtained from the visitor center near the ferry. Bumboats leave from Changi Point once there are enough people on board.

Malaysia and Indonesia
Regular ferry services also operate between Singapore and the Malaysian resort island of Tioman, as well as the nearby Indonesian islands of Batam and Bintan.

RULES AND REGULATIONS
Visa
For a stay of up to thirty days a visa is not required for visitors with passports issued by North and South American and European countries, excluding former member states of the USSR.

Travelers with passports from other countries should check with the Singapore government Web site (www.gov.sg) or the local Singapore consulate for visa requirements. In all cases six months' validity on your passport is required. In addition, travelers should have round-trip tickets and sufficient funds for their stay in Singapore.

Drugs

Trafficking in all but the smallest quantity of narcotics is punishable by death on conviction.

Driving

A valid driver's license from your own country or a valid international driver's license is required for driving in Singapore.

Fines

Singapore has been dubbed "Fine City." Smoking is not permitted in public service vehicles, museums, libraries, elevators, theaters, cinemas, air-conditioned restaurants, hair salons, supermarkets, department stores, and government offices. There are tough fines for offenders. Other civil offenses that incur fines include jaywalking, littering, urinating in an elevator, not flushing a public toilet, and chewing gum!

MONEY

There is no restriction on the amount of currency you can bring in, and major credit and charge cards are widely accepted.

The local currency is Singapore dollars and cents. U.S. dollars and British pounds are also accepted in most major shopping centers and big department stores.

Banking hours are Monday to Friday, 10:00 a.m. to 3:00 p.m.; Saturday, 9:30 a.m. to 1:00 p.m. (some banks are open until 3:00 p.m.); and Sunday, 9:30 a.m. to 3:00 p.m. (some banks in Orchard Road).

Most banks handle traveler's checks and change foreign currency. Passports are required when cashing traveler's checks. A commission may be charged.

Apart from banks and hotels, money can be changed wherever the sign "licensed money changer" is displayed, which applies to most shopping complexes. Visitors are discouraged from changing money with unlicensed money changers.

SAFETY

Singapore's reputation as a safe and secure destination is well known, and it enjoys one of the lowest crime rates in the world.

SHOPPING

Of course, no visit to Singapore would be complete without a shopping trip or two, or three, and one of these expeditions must include a visit to Orchard Road. This legendary street got its name from the many nutmeg and pepper plantations that lined the streets until the early years of the twentieth century, when a mysterious disease totally wiped them out. How very different Orchard Road looks today: here you will be spoiled for choice. Large department stores, shopping malls, and exclusive boutiques offer a range of international products as well as Asian artifacts, furniture, Persian carpets, jewelry, table linen, silks, batiks, and the latest electronic goods. Despite the heat and humidity you can shop in comfort, as the malls and shops are all air-conditioned and many of them are interlinked. However, if you are interested in bargains and lower prices in general, hop on to the efficient MRT to one of the suburbs and experience shopping like the locals. Nearly every housing estate has its shopping center with a variety of shops, from the humble corner store to elegant designer label shops.

The Great Singapore Sale

The Great Singapore sale takes place in the run up to National Day. Every shop in Singapore has a month of sales, usually in June or July. To pick up a designer label at a bargain price, go to stores that sell last season's stock or overruns at discount prices. Your hotel and the local newspaper are the places to ask and look for what's available and where. You could possibly do the same at the leading department stores such as Robinsons or Tangs.

The latter is a perfect example of a Chinese rags-to-riches story. Over forty years ago, a former lace peddler, C. K. Tang, had the foresight to see that the site now opposite the Orchard MRT Station would become a bustling thoroughfare. He subsequently brought building materials from his home in Swatow province in China and started constructing a department store. In 1982 the site was redeveloped and now contains not only a department store but also a high-rise hotel. However, it was rebuilt in the traditional Chinese style, with a green roof and red pillars, and Tangs is recognized today as a leading home-grown department store selling the best of local fashion and design.

Sales Tax

Most shops levy a 5 percent Goods and Services Tax (GST), but the good news is that you may be eligible for a refund when you leave Singapore if your purchases exceed $300 and if you get the shop to complete the necessary documentation. Look out for the Tax Free Shopping sticker.

Shopping Hours

Shops are usually open from 10:00 or 11:00 a.m. until 9:00 or 10:00 p.m., and are open on public holidays as well. So there is no excuse not to "shop till you drop."

NIGHTLIFE

Singapore does not spring to life after dark as, say, Bangkok or Hong Kong do. Bars and nightclubs exist, but anyone in search of racier forms of nightlife is likely to be disappointed. One of Singapore's most famous night sights used to be Bugis Street, where gorgeous transvestites would promenade and noisy bars would stay open until the early hours, but the area disappeared in 1985 when it was bulldozed to make way for the MRT. However, in true Singapore style, a sanitized version of Bugis Street has been re-created, with closed-circuit TV and plainclothes police to ensure that soliciting does not occur. Where there are transvestites, these have been hired as "customer relations officers" to explain the history of the area to the visiting public.

Nightclubs are increasing in number and quality, however, in response to the growing demands of young and relatively wealthy Singaporeans, as well as the expatriate community and tourists. Cover charges are fairly expensive and the dress code is conservative smart casual. Most clubs will close around midnight during the week, although as you would expect they stay open until the early hours on the weekend.

Bars not only have a more relaxed dress code,

but have extended happy hours, which certainly helps the visitor on a tight budget, as alcoholic drinks are expensive. In order to counter its rather staid reputation, Singapore recently lifted the ban on bar top dancing and now allows pubs to stay open all night.

Boat Quay and Clarke Quay on the Singapore River are both lively places full of restaurants and bars where alfresco dining is popular. In the middle of the nineteenth century, Boat Quay was the center of the Singapore River's commercial life, but a hundred years later the area had fallen on hard times. The government, realizing that it was in danger of over-sanitizing Singapore, decided to restore some of its historical charm. The façades were retained and restored, and new eating places and watering holes quickly opened up. Harry's Bar on Boat Quay has become famous, or perhaps infamous, as the bar where Nick Leeson, the trader who brought down Barings Bank, used to hang out. It offers food and live jazz, available in equal measure.

Further up the river is Clarke Quay. Again, this has been renovated, but it has a different atmosphere from Boat Quay, being more geared to families. On Sunday there is a lively flea market here.

CULTURE

All the various ethnic groups in Singapore have formed cultural societies to maintain and sustain their identities, and here music and dance play important roles. The playing of the *sitar*, the classical Indian stringed instrument, the staging of colorful operas from Canton, Hokkien, and Teochew, and the magical sound of the Malay *gamelan*, a native version of the Indonesian ensemble of gong and chimes, all contribute to a vibrant cultural life. Every June there is month-long Festival of Arts. In addition there is an annual film festival and regular productions of live theater.

Furthermore, because of its colonial background, Western ballet and classical music have a large local following, and the city is a regular stopping-off point for performing arts companies touring East and Southeast Asia. It is easy to dip your toe into the varied waters of Singapore's cultural life. You can find out what is going on in the English-language newspapers (look in the *Straits Times)* or at your hotel, which will help to arrange the tickets.

Well worth visiting are the Singapore Art Museum, particularly for its outstanding collection of contemporary Asian art, the National Museum, and the Esplanade, a huge new integrated arts complex on the waterfront east of the Padang, home to the Theaters on the Bay, (popularly known as the Durians, after the fruit, because of their shape). This bold project reflects the government's drive to foster a unified Singaporean culture.

chapter seven

BANQUETS & ENTERTAINING

All business as well as most social entertaining is done in restaurants. Banquets are a feature of Chinese business life and the celebration of major family events. Guests often arrive late so as not to appear greedy and, since Singapore is a hierarchical society, they often arrive in order of rank. The banquet will usually take place in a private dining room in a hotel or restaurant.

EATING ETIQUETTE

The solitary diner is a rare sight in Singapore. Eating is a communal event in all ethnic groups, although the manner of dining differs. For the Malays, Indians, and Straits Chinese, eating with your fingers is the only true way to enjoy curry. However, only the right hand is used because,

among traditional Hindus and Muslims, the left
hand is reserved for personal hygiene. Even then
only the tips of the fingers of the right hand are
used, and it is considered most impolite to touch
another person's food with your fingers. When
helping yourself from a communal dish always
use the serving spoon provided. Diners wash their
hands before the meal, and you may find yourself
being offered a bowl of warm water and a napkin
both before and after a meal in finer Indian or
Malay restaurants. Even in the most basic of
establishments you will often see a row of wash
basins provided for the use of their customers.

For the Chinese, dining etiquette is somewhat
different as the use of chopsticks is the norm.
There are certain straightforward rules governing
their use. For instance, never put your chopsticks
upright in a bowl of rice as it symbolizes death. It
is also considered to be bad manners to wave your
chopsticks about, point them at somebody, or
make a noise with them (although it is more
than acceptable to drink soup noisily or
slurp noodles). It is permissible, from
time to time, to rest one's
chopsticks on the rest stand,
never across the dinner plate
or rice bowl. It is bad
manners to reach across another person's
chopsticks in order to get at the food on display.

Unlike the West, guests do not stay long chatting and drinking coffee after the end of the meal. When everyone has finished eating, that really is the end of the festivities and usually all the guests leave at the same time.

For the Malays, forks and spoons will usually be provided for a meal, but not knives as these are considered to be weapons. However, do not worry as any meat will already have been cut up into bite-sized portions. The fork is held in the left hand and used to push the food on to the spoon. It is considered impolite to make a noise with a spoon when serving yourself, and you should always ask your host to join you in eating. The Malays are delighted if you take second helpings and, unlike the Chinese, do not think you are being greedy, so you do not have to protest when offered more, but graciously accept. On the other hand, it is considered rude to refuse food, so at least try to sample a small piece when served. If you absolutely cannot eat the food proffered you should invent a good excuse, such as an allergy.

SEATING ARRANGEMENTS

Typically the table will be round with a revolving central platform for the dishes, so the whole group can see, speak to each other, and help themselves to food without interruption. The place of honor, unlike in the West, is on the left side of the host. The more junior guests sit with their backs to the front entrance. This comes from the time when it was feared that armed assailants could burst into a room and attack those nearest the door first. However relaxed the evening is there will always be a seating plan, and so one waits to be seated. Of course, the host does not take his seat until everyone else has taken theirs.

So as not to be seen to be bragging about the evening's fare, the host will probably say a few words about the paucity and insignificance of the food on offer. The guests respond to this humble stance by admiring the food as it appears, discussing with fellow guests the subtle flavoring and composition of each dish. Usually a banquet consists of eight or ten courses and the dishes appear one at a time. The use of chopsticks is *de rigueur* at an event like this, but in the home many Chinese use forks, spoons, and plates.

MAKING SPEECHES AND PROPOSING TOASTS

In order not to spoil the enjoyment of the food, all speeches are made before the banquet begins.

To commence the proceedings
the host will raise his glass and
propose a toast, or simply say
"*Ch'ing.*" The other guests similarly raise
their glasses, holding the glass in both
hands, the fingers of the right hand under
its bottom, the left hand holding it. There can be
further toasts throughout the meal when each
new course appears.

It is a good idea to pace yourself at a banquet,
or you risk being overwhelmed by the time the
last dish appears. You are not obliged to eat a lot
of any food you do not like, but you should eat
whatever you serve yourself. Always take the food
from the dish nearest to you on the revolving
circular table top.

RECIPROCATING

It is part of doing business in Singapore to be
entertained and to entertain in return, and even
though your own country might be far less
formal, Singaporeans will usually feel more
comfortable if entertained "Singapore style."
Whether the "return match" is at home or in
Singapore, the same basic rules apply.

First, the hotel or restaurant chosen should be
of sufficiently high standing and reputation to
impress your guests. Second, the function will

need to be held in a private dining room. When considering the menu, it is a good idea to establish whether any of your guests are Singaporean Malays or Indians as the menu will need to reflect this. Muslims do not eat pork or drink alcohol and Indians are often vegetarian.

If you are entertaining in Singapore take local advice as to the suitability of the venue, the menu, and the number of courses that would be appropriate. It is important to get help with the seating plan—and name place cards, with correct spellings and title, of course—in this hierarchical society. The Western practice of "sit anywhere" causes great confusion and embarrassment. You as the host will need to be there in plenty of time, not only to greet your guests but also to check that everything is in order.

Arranging this in your home territory might prove a little more difficult. It is always sensible to play it safe and entertain in a Chinese restaurant, albeit one of excellent standing. Singaporeans will feel at home in such a place, and if any of the team is Malay or Indian, the restaurant will be able to provide suitable vegetarian dishes. Chinese restaurants in the West are, of course, familiar with private dining rooms, and will nearly always have one or be prepared to screen off part of the restaurant for the visiting party. You might wish to dine in the chosen restaurant beforehand to see if it and the service are up to the mark, and then later spend some time talking to the management about your requirements for the meal. A careful and methodical approach pays handsome dividends, as your guests will realize that you have gone to a lot of trouble on their behalf and will be suitably impressed.

How Not to Do It

The senior managers of a Western company inadvertently entertained their Singaporean colleagues in the worst possible way. The hosts chose a very prestigious hotel with a splendid private dining room, but after this things went from bad to worse.

First, they had drinks before dinner, not realizing that Singaporeans feel distinctly unhappy drinking without food, and do not like to eat too late either.

The menu was chosen with care, but with no thought as to the requirements of their guests. The main course was rare roast beef. Singaporean Chinese do not like eating large pieces of meat, let alone eating it rare, and as for the Malays and Indians, it was a disaster.

Dessert followed in the same vein. Singaporeans always have fresh fruit sliced into small portions, but on this occasion a large chocolate pudding was served. This was far too rich for the guests, and as for the cheese course that followed, Singaporeans as a rule dislike dairy products.

The meal finished with coffee, and each guest was given a present of an unwrapped ball point pen with the logo of the host company.

The entire occasion was an example of how not to entertain Singaporeans. Fortunately, despite the *faux pas,* the business relationship did not founder, and eventually after a more appropriate meal, a deal beneficial to both parties was signed!

chapter eight

BUSINESS BRIEFING

THE ECONOMIC MIRACLE

The initial business advantage of the island came from its location on the shortest route for ships

between the Indian Ocean and China and Japan. This coupled with free-trade colonialism and an influx of immigrants liberated from the constraints of their homelands gave the country an environment for economic growth.

When Singapore became independent it was a small territory with no natural resources, and a poor, unskilled workforce. Lee Kuan Yew and Finance Minister Goh Keng Swee set out a development strategy with the state as principal investor in an export-oriented free-market system.

However, within a few short years, Britain announced its withdrawal from the military base that contributed 20 percent to the island's GDP.

This was a massive blow, but in some ways it was a blessing in disguise as it forced Singapore to stand on its own two feet and to seek competitive advantage by converting the old British naval base into the world's third-largest commercial port.

The island's manufacturing and industrial base was expanded by attracting technologically strong foreign companies with various tax incentives. The government controlled industrial financing and development, and invested heavily in education. The result in the late 1960s was double-digit GDP growth.

In the early 1970s government policies to expand trade and industry and attract foreign investment paid off. Singapore managed to ride out the 1973 oil crisis with slower but, nonetheless, single-digit growth. Tariff protection for the electrical and electronic sectors was reduced and financial services became a focus for growth. By 1975, Singapore was the world's third-largest oil-refining location and its third-busiest port, and five years later it became Asia's most important financial center after Tokyo and Hong Kong. The government then targeted computer technology and electronics as the next phase in Singapore's industrial development.

Singapore weathered the 1997 Asian financial crisis, but its export dependence caused a recession in 2001-2. Competition from China spurs the government to seek trade alliances and economic restructuring. Today the U.S.A. remains its single largest trading partner, followed by Malaysia, Hong Kong, and Japan.

Singapore's success since independence has rested on its recognition that it needs to retain a regional competitive advantage against countries such as China. It has sought to do this by adapting its work and management styles and by investing in education, skills, and technology. This has been reinforced by the ease of entry for foreign investment in a corruption-free stable economy. Singapore is also pressing for an ASEAN Free Trade Zone and seeking to create bilateral free-trade arrangements with Australia, Canada, Japan, and the United States.

FINANCIAL MANAGEMENT

Initially the Singapore government tied its currency to the U.S. dollar but by the late 1970s the currency had been floated and all controls on currency exchange abolished.

Singapore's compulsory Central Provident Fund, founded in 1955, deposits a predetermined portion of worker income into a tax-exempt account, which the employer matches. The Fund, which covers worker retirement and disability, also creates consistent budget surpluses and a national savings rate of nearly 50 percent of GDP.

The 1997 Asian financial crisis inflated Singapore's prime lending rate to nearly 8 percent and devalued its dollar slightly against the U.S. dollar. Debt-free status helped Singapore recover quickly. The lending rate soon fell back to 6 percent, and huge foreign reserves—the world's largest in per capita terms—cushion the dollar.

In the last few years the devaluation of other Asian currencies has eroded Singapore's competitiveness. With virtually no official controls on the movement of capital, Singapore cannot use monetary policy to stimulate or suppress its economic activity. The government has consequently opted to cut business costs by reducing employer contributions to the Central Provident Fund rather than attempt to devalue the currency.

Singapore trades in shares, bonds, derivatives, and commodities twenty-four hours a day and so overlaps with the trading hours in both the U.S.A. and Europe. The financial institutions range from insurance to investment banking to providing services targeted at the expatriate community.

It is all too easy in commerce and industry for the visitor to be seduced by the Western dress,

behavior, and excellent English of those around
you to think you are in a Western country and
revert to your home behavior. You should not!
When doing business in Singapore it is vital to be
aware of what is considered acceptable conduct.

BUILDING RELATIONSHIPS

Time is needed to build a Singaporean business
relationship, as it is founded on trust and mutual
respect. Once established, it is worth its weight in
gold. Do not plunge into business when first
beginning a meeting. Singaporeans, like other
Asians, prefer to get to know the person they are
dealing with; after all, he or she is the personal
face of the company at the moment. Take time to
show them that you are a reliable person. Business
relationships are based on honor and
integrity. Take the trouble not only to
establish contacts but to maintain them.
Trusted networking or *guangxi* has been
the main way of getting anything done in
China and Singapore for decades.
Although *guangxi* is usually based on
family, school, and university ties, because of the
obligation that members owe each other, non-
Singaporeans can enter this "magic circle" if they
are able to demonstrate that they are trustworthy,
and this in turn can open up trading networks in

Singapore and further afield in Southeast Asia.

Finally the important thing to remember about business relationships is that they must be nurtured with both direct and indirect contact. A failure to do so will expose your business to attack from competitors.

INTRODUCTIONS

People in Singapore do not look directly into the eyes of the person they are meeting as this is a sign of disrespect. This can be disconcerting when you first experience it and it is certainly not a sign of shiftiness!

The normal verbal exchange on introduction is to express pleasure at meeting. If business enters the conversation in any way the discussion should be modest. Do not talk up your business.

When introducing people the etiquette is always to mention higher before lower rank, older before younger, and a woman before a man (unlike the rest of Asia, except for Hong Kong).

The handshake is the normal business introduction between members of the same sex but not between opposite sexes. If a woman wishes to shake hands with a man she must make the move, and only do it on introduction. The handshake should be soft and linger a while. Crushing bones and vigorously shaking the arm of the other person is not done!

It is important not to draw conclusions from how a person looks at you or shakes your hand when you first meet, as the etiquette is totally different from that in the West.

SMALL TALK

Good topics of polite conversation are positive things about Singapore, including how well it is developing, how wonderful the food is, how attractive the scenery, how you are enjoying your stay. Always start meetings, even if you know the person, with five minutes of general discussion before plunging into the agenda. To do otherwise is to set the wrong tone for the discussions ahead.

Bad topics are anything critical of Singapore or its government, or anything about sex, religion, and politics.

HANDS

Within the Chinese community items such as gifts, including *Hong Bao* money and business cards, are given and accepted with two hands. With Malays and Indians never use the left hand for handling food, money, gifts, shaking hands, giving business cards, or any other transaction.

When using your right hand, remember not to

point at a person; rather use the whole of the
right hand, palm upward, in a gesturing motion.
When ordering a taxi, simply turn the palm
down, beckoning toward yourself.

BUSINESS CARDS

Because the Singapore business environment is so
hierarchical it is important to note a person's
position in a company. For this reason business
cards are crucial. When you receive them you will
notice that one side is written in English and the
other in Chinese. Take a minute or two to study
them; not only is this being courteous to the giver
but, importantly, it lets you know the position
and authority of that person in their company.
Have your card printed in both Chinese and
English and take local advice as to the most
appropriate title to put on it. This is necessary to
ensure that you get to meet the right people in the
company you are visiting. Even though you might
be a little embarrassed at your high-sounding
title, it has been recommended for a good reason.

When handing out business cards, you should
give them to everyone present, using both hands,
with the print facing the recipient so that it can be
read easily. Never put a card in your back pocket
or write on someone's business card. Both actions
will give offense.

MEETINGS

It is important to be well prepared and to plan business discussions in great detail before meetings. Not only is punctuality vital, but it is a good idea to arrive fifteen minutes before the scheduled time. Members of a team might come from different ethnic groups, and so, although the Chinese will shake hands upon greeting, Muslims and Malays may prefer salaams, that is, putting their hands together and giving a slight bow saying "*salaam*," or "peace." Similarly, Hindus might use the same form saying "*namaste*." Business meetings are usually conducted in English.

Tea is always served at meetings and it is polite to accept it. You will notice that the seating is hierarchical and the visitor will be seated next to the host. Dress is usually more formal than it would be in the office and shorts are most definitely not worn. Expect meetings to be rather slow. Although the Chinese issue agendas and stick to them, they tend to have a rather verbose negotiating style; also, in Asia generally it is considered important and polite to pause for about fifteen seconds before answering a question or considering a statement. This is longer than is the norm in the West, but it does not mean that the feeling is negative. Singaporeans look for "how" you say things as well as "what" you say, and decision-making happens slowly. If all this seems a little daunting, remember that once made, decisions will hold good for the long term, and Asian businesspeople do not like being rushed into hasty decisions.

Be patient and allow time for reflection. It is also a good idea to restate your position several times if necessary because polite persistence pays off. Never, of course, let frustration make you lose your temper. A warm, friendly attitude emphasizing common aims will be much more constructive. Remember the golden rule that throughout Asia "yes" does not necessarily mean "I agree"—it is more like "I hear you." Chinese speakers tend to use an indirect style, hinting rather than telling, and sometimes smile to avoid embarrassment when giving bad news.

Always end your meetings with a summary of what was discussed, what was agreed upon, and what actions are to be carried out and by whom.

WOMEN IN BUSINESS

Women are well represented in the professions, commerce, and industry, with many holding senior managerial positions. Western business visitors should always observe Singaporean protocols where dress, behavior in the office, and

144

body language are concerned; any sign of flirting could destroy the woman's position and certainly ruin a business deal. Singaporean women tend to dress conservatively and, despite the hot, humid climate, upper arms are always covered and knee-length skirts are the norm. In more formal offices women often wear pantyhose, but not in more relaxed establishments.

SAVING FACE

The all-important issue of "saving face" applies to all three ethnic groups. The point to remember here is that saving face—as with everything in Singapore—is not just about individuals but about the group to which they belong. Losing face is not just a matter of personal embarrassment: it undermines an individual's integrity and moral character. More than that, it undermines the whole group. Most importantly, saving face preserves the group's harmony, whether the group at the time is the family, one's work colleagues, or the nation itself. To embarrass somebody totally or make them lose face is one of the worst mistakes a foreign visitor can make. Asians have long memories. The person who has brought about this loss of face will be regarded as shallow and lacking in personal integrity, and therefore not to be trusted.

So it is important not to blunder inadvertently into this potential minefield. Be very careful about criticism and strong disagreement. If it is essential to be critical, then do so subtly and with tact. When disagreeing with someone, try to nudge them gently in the other direction. Never think that you are being too subtle, for a Singaporean will always get the hint and even respect you for being so aware of the cultural differences between Asia and the West.

Never rebuke a senior in front of a junior, or ask a junior's opinion in front of a senior, or openly praise just one member of the group without including the group as a whole. Within the group they will know who deserves the praise.

Losing one's temper is also seen as a "loss of face," as is any other display of strong emotion—a person who is out of control or reveals their emotions too easily cannot be trusted.

NEGOTIATING STYLES

In Singapore successful outcomes with a partner, customer, or supplier are more likely and certainly easier if you can appreciate how the person across the table or at the other end of the telephone or e-mail is thinking about the business opportunity or the problem to be solved. Asians do not think just in terms of cause and effect, one thing leading to another, but rather in terms of their network of intuitive and intricate relationships and the thought patterns that go with them. The Westerner often enjoys talking about the problem and then the solutions. The Asian wants to know the benefits, certainly the financial benefits but also the impact on relationships within his or her organization and the wider world.

A focus on the benefits of any deal or arrangement and on the common ground cannot be stressed too highly. Where there are problems the Asian mind will be prepared to share the burden and will expect this to cut both ways, irrespective of any contractual terms. If there are other existing relationships that will be disadvantaged by the deal, it is well to look for ways of mitigation to ease the mind of the person you are negotiating with. This might mean the arrangements are not as clean-cut as you would like, but it is more likely that the deal will fly, especially if the damage is done to someone who has many dealings with the person you are negotiating with.

Any weaknesses you have will be exploited in attempts to reach a decision—disclose them at your peril, even if it means that you have to catch the nine o'clock plane home. Know your walking away point, hold to this, and do not make early concessions. Stress the package nature of any concession you offer—there must be something in return. Refer to the pressure you are having from the head office or senior management if you are close to a deal and are having difficulty in closing.

The benefits of having a Singaporean as part of your team are enormous. Not only will they pick up shades of meaning that have passed you by, but they will also discover in the meeting, or more likely outside, the crucial issues to be resolved to reach a settlement.

DECISION MAKING

It is important to know who the decision maker is and what his needs are if it is not the person sitting opposite you. Because the Asian commitment is not just to a contract that has been pored over by the lawyers, but to a relationship, reaching decisions can be slow. However, implementation in Singapore is fast once everything is agreed to.

If a decision seems difficult to achieve, be prepared to table and discuss the benefits and disadvantages to your side as well as the other person, and show how the deal is fair if not ideal.

The one comfort in doing business in Singapore is that it is easier than most Asian countries to negotiate and reach a decision, and that there are no "commissions" or any other side payments to be made once a deal is reached.

CONTRACTS AND FULFILLMENT

Both sides expect contracts to be honored and fulfilled. However, the nature of business in Asia is that, in the event of trouble, whether it be escalating raw material costs or a decline in demand, the problem is expected to be shared. Cooperation and flexibility mean that one does not follow the small print of the contract to the letter.

E-mail Contact

Even when you know someone very well it is best to avoid using e-mail except for the exchange of factual data. Once into the area of ideas or concepts or proposals all sorts of misinterpretations are possible in the shorthand style that is so convenient for other purposes.

TEAM BUILDING

Finally we turn to teams and teamwork. As in other areas of life and work in Singapore, seniority as well as professionalism is very important. The team leader makes the decisions after lengthy consultation with the group, so that every member is on board with the decision. Thereafter the team leader demands implicit obedience and it would be unthinkable for a member of the team to complain about the decision. Harmony, again, is all important, and because of this working practice tends to be slow and methodical. The length of the process can sometimes frustrate foreign managers who are used to more rapid decision making, but even so they appreciate the wisdom of taking the time to reach a decision that is fully supported.

The team leader is responsible not only for selecting its members, but for giving clear, concise instructions, emphasizing the collective nature of the enterprise, making certain that everyone is occupied, and regularly monitoring the team's progress. An effective team leader will be aware that a smile does not equal satisfaction, and perhaps more importantly that a statement of agreement does not necessarily mean that a person understands. It is essential to give face to everyone and certainly never criticize a senior in front of the whole team. Only ever comment on poor performance in private. A diligent manager will give encouragement and praise where it is due, but remember to praise the whole team and not single out a particular member, thereby causing embarrassment and loss of face.

COMMUNICATING

TELECOMMUNICATIONS

There are two telecom companies in Singapore offering the full data and voice, broadband/multimedia, and e-service range. They are SingTel, with hubs in Singapore and Australia, and StarHub, owned by Singapore Technologies (ST) and the global players BT and NTT.

The international dialing code for Singapore is 0065, but once inside Singapore you will not need any special area dialing codes. However, Singapore has recently added the prefix 6 to all landlines so, if you were given a number some time ago and are having trouble getting through, this could well be the reason.

Local calls in Singapore cost very little: they are practically free from private phones and cost 10 cents from public phones for three minutes. Many people now use card phones instead of pay phones as well as credit-card phones. Phone cards are widely available from post offices, *bureaux de change*, pharmacies, bookstores, and shops such as 7 Eleven. International phone cards are also widely available.

If you want to use your mobile phone while in Singapore it is a good idea to check with your provider as to how to do this and how much it will cost.

THE INTERNET

Apart from the telecom companies, the other Internet providers are Pacific Internet, the Asia-wide provider, and Reddweb. The easiest and cheapest way to contact friends and family while in Singapore is to use the Internet, and it is practical to sign up for a free Internet e-mail address that you can use anywhere. There are many Internet cafés where you can easily get a line and, as this is Singapore, most hotels offer in-room modems to their guests. In fact, with over 150 hotspots in the city, getting online at broadband speeds could not be easier.

For those who are going to spend more than a few days in the country, the most useful Web site for information is www.expatsingapore.com.

THE MEDIA

The two media groups are SPH (Singapore Press Holdings) and MediaCorp (Media Corporation of Singapore), which publish newspapers and magazines, broadcast on TV, and have comprehensive Web sites and online editions. MediaCorp also has radio stations. SPH only recently became a broadcaster and MediaCorp similarly only recently entered the newspaper business.

Newspapers and Magazines

Daily newspapers are available in all four official languages, and in English there are the *Straits Times*, the *Business Times*, and the afternoon tabloid the *New Paper*, all owned by SPH, and *Today* owned by MediaCorp.

The *Straits Times* has a broad coverage of local, regional, and international news and its excellent Web site (www.straitstimes.asia1.com.sg) gives the visitor an opportunity to get up to date with the latest news and events. The *Business Times* (www.business-times.asia1.com.sg) covers the commercial and financial issues in much the same way, while the tabloid *New Paper* is purely for local consumption, as a visit to its Web site (www.newpaper.asia1.com.sg) will demonstrate. *Today* (www.todayonline.com) is positioned as a mid-market alternative to the SPH offerings.

All papers are sensitive to the government line on major issues and are not controversial.

Of the local magazines, the glossy *Vogue Singapore* will give you an insight and perhaps a taste for the more exclusive side of the island's life.

The international press and magazines are well represented on the newsstands but will disappear if something offends the country's sensitivities or its government.

TV and Radio

All four languages are catered to by MediaCorp and the channels to watch in English are Channel 5 and NewsAsia, while SPH broadcasts TV in Chinese and with the English-language Channel i.

Turning the FM dial will bring you the MediaCorp stations with Gold at 90.5 with news and music, classical music on Symphony at 92.4, NewsRadio at 93.8, old to new hits at Class 95.0, and the latest on Perfect at 98.7.

POSTAL SERVICES

Mail is usually delivered by the next working day at some time in early to late afternoon through a network of more than 1,300 postal outlets around the island. Singapore addresses use a six-digit postal code and the basic mail service is run by Singapore Post (SP), a subsidiary of SingTel. SP has the exclusive right to provide basic mail service (letters and postcards) until 2007. Express services (small packets, printed papers, and parcels) have been opened up to competition, and many courier companies offer such services to local and international destinations. The international courier companies such as DHL, Fedex, UPS, and TNT are all found in the city.

In addition Singapore has some distinctive services and these include:

Express LUM, to send urgent local mail anywhere on the island on a same-day basis.

SAMs (self-service automated machines) dotted around the island. Here you can weigh postal items, pay fines and telephone/utility bills, and buy stamps at any time, day or night.

Speedpost, an SP international courier service up to 21 kg.

Fastfreight, an SP door-to-door delivery service that sends urgent heavy shipments (over 21 kg) to more than 125 countries worldwide.

LANGUAGES
In 1965 great consideration was given to the question of which language should be the official one in the new polyglot nation. With three distinctive ethnic groups, it was a highly sensitive issue, especially as racial tensions often threatened

to explode over minor issues, and, in some cases, actually did so.

In 1959, when Singapore attained self-government, it was all very straightforward: Malay was declared the official language in order to prepare the way for entry into the Federation of Malaysia. All that changed after August 9, 1965, because the Singaporean government realized that if it continued with Malay as the official language the country would not be able to make a living as an international trading community, which was imperative if the new nation were to survive. The Singaporean Chinese now actively promoted Chinese as the new official language, their cultural, business, and civic leaders pointing out to Lee Kuan Yew's government that it was the language spoken by more than 80 percent of the population. The Chinese, understandably, felt proud of their language and culture, and indeed in the 1950s all classes of Chinese in Singapore— from businessmen to rickshaw drivers—gave money toward the founding of a Chinese-language university in Singapore that was named "Nantah," which soon became the symbol of Chinese culture and values, language and education.

It seemed to follow that Chinese would become the official language. However, Lee Kuan Yew had other ideas and he concluded that the least divisive solution to this problem would be to have four official languages: Malay, Mandarin Chinese, Tamil, and English. In this way, no one ethnic group would have a linguistic advantage.

Malay was to be the language of administration. But it was not the use of Tamil or Malay as official languages that angered the Chinese community: it was the introduction of English as an official language, especially as it was to be taught in all schools in addition to a child's ethnic language, that was considered a betrayal. Indeed, Lee Kuan Yew and his government were portrayed as "pseudo foreigners who forget their ancestors" in one of the leading Chinese newspapers.

Singapore, however, had a history of excellence in the teaching of subjects in the English language—it had been the regional center for education in English. It had good schools, arts and science colleges, and teacher-training and medical colleges. The brightest English-educated students from Malaya and Borneo, as well as the former Dutch East Indies (which later became Indonesia), attended these colleges and trained as doctors, teachers, and other professionals as well as administrators. The opposition to English as one of the common languages was unremitting, especially at Nantah. Eventually, in 1978, Lee Kuan Yew persuaded this institution to make English the language of instruction. The majority of the Chinese-speaking parents accepted this change as inevitable, as did the students—especially because graduates were having great difficulty in finding employment compared to their fellow students who had been educated in English at the University of Singapore. Although it was a painful adjustment for Nantah to make, by the early 1990s Nantah and the University of Singapore felt confident enough to merge and become the National University of Singapore, or NUS as it is now known.

However, the language debate was still not over—although this time it was the status of the Chinese language or, more precisely, the different Chinese dialects that are still spoken in Singapore reflecting the many regions where the immigrants originated. The predominant ones are Hokkien, Hakka, Hainanese, Hoklo, Hokchiu, and, to a lesser extent, Cantonese (the latter being the dialect spoken in Hong Kong). From the 1980s onward, Prime Minister Lee Kuan Yew encouraged the speaking of Mandarin in the home because he realized it would be easier for children to master it at school if they were not burdened by dialects. He therefore stopped making speeches in his native Hokkien, and TV and radio program makers were no longer permitted to broadcast in Chinese dialects, only in Mandarin. To encourage the speaking of the language the Prime Minister instituted a "speak Mandarin" day once a month.

At first, the insistence on the use of Mandarin was seen by many Singaporean Chinese as something of an academic exercise: all very well in theory, but making no difference to the practical issues of the day, such as making money. However, the opening up of China, whose official language has always been Mandarin, brought about a swift change of attitude. It soon became

clear that those in the workforce, whether professional or technical, could command a premium if they spoke Mandarin as well as English. The handing back of Hong Kong to China in 1997 further underlined the importance of Mandarin because the Singaporean Chinese could see their fellow

overseas Chinese rather reluctantly having to embrace it. They realized that the way forward in the newly enlarged China would be by using Mandarin, because the Beijing government regarded all regional dialects as grossly inferior to it. Mandarin has always been the language of government and administration, whether Imperial or Communist, and, indeed, for centuries the sign of an educated person was that he spoke Mandarin.

Singlish

The Singaporeans have developed their own way of speaking English, known as "Singlish." This is a usage that has its roots in Chinese grammatical structure. Thus the Singlish "You follow me" means "We go together." "Can or not?" means "Will you or won't you?" Moreover, Singaporeans often mix ethnic terms with English words to create more colorful expressions when they feel that the Chinese or Malay word better describes what they want to say.

The government, on the other hand, wants English to be the common bond between all Singaporeans and opposes anything that it sees as the "dumbing down" of the English language, and so, from time to time, it instigates a "speak proper English" campaign.

To the untrained ear, listening to a conversation in rapid "Singaporean" is highly confusing and totally illogical. Overleaf are some examples.

SOME SINGAPOREAN PHRASES

Boh-chup from the Hokkien meaning "could not be bothered/could not care less" e.g., "Ah, boh-chup—I didn't win the lottery."

Havoc from the English "disorder," or "confusion," but used here as an adjective: "My son is so havoc he doesn't do his homework and wants to go to clubs!"

Kayu from the Malay meaning "stupid": "My son is so kayu, he always gets poor grades at school."

Lah a Malay prefix used to emphasize something, as in: "He can do it lah, no problem," or "No lah," meaning "no way."

Maama from the Tamil word for uncle, so a "Maama shop" is an Indian/English word meaning a shop run by an Indian merchant.

Obiang from the Hokkien word meaning ugly: "That dress is so obiang."

Uwee this is derived from Australian slang meaning a "U-turn": "I'll have to do a uwee."

Waah! has no precise meaning, but is an exclamation of excitement and amazement. This word is frequently heard at banquets as each new dish appears.

Even when using the English language, which we know has been taught in Singapore schools for over thirty years, mistakes and confusion can arise. If you find the way in which something is said upsetting, remember that for none of the ethnic groups is English their first language, and even when speaking it they will often still use their own grammatical structure. Something that would be perfectly polite in Chinese can sound abrupt and offensive when translated literally into English. For example, in the West we say to a guest "Would you like a cup of tea?" In Singapore this becomes "You want to drink tea or not?"!

Similarly, in Chinese and Malay there are no tense changes, they simply use a time phrase to indicate past or future. Again, to a foreigner this can sound very uneducated when it is directly translated into English. For example, "I see that movie already with my friend."

The tip here is to be culturally sensitive and not immediately to jump to the conclusion that somebody is being deliberately rude. Learn to tolerate ambiguity, and accept a degree of frustration in order to deal with the different circumstances you will encounter.

BODY LANGUAGE

Westerners often find it difficult to read a
Singaporean's body language, although they have
no problem in understanding their Western
counterparts, who are used to being more direct.
Westerners may find it difficult to conceal anger,
frustration, boredom, or tiredness, and recognize
these signs in others. However, in a culture where
harmony is promoted and people do not want to
give bad news, body language can be much more
difficult to interpret. We have seen in the chapter
on business that in all three ethnic groups "Yes"
does not necessarily mean "I agree." If there is a
slight pause, an embarrassed smile, or a sucking
through the teeth, this probably means that "Yes"
is "No." The Indian community adds another
dimension to body language in the matter of
"Yes" and "No." An Indian will wag his head,
which to the Westerner can look like a "No," when
he is actually replying in the affirmative.

In China, you might encounter loud belching
after a meal, or spitting in the street, but not nose-
blowing. You should be aware that all these
actions are considered equally disgusting in
Singapore, by all groups. If you have a cold and
need to blow your nose, you should excuse
yourself from the present company and go to the
bathroom to do so. You might notice that there
are large handkerchiefs for sale in the shops, but

these are intended for mopping your brow in the most humid months.

HUMOR

Humor, especially British humor, does not work well as it relies heavily on puns and is often self-deprecating. So, if a Singaporean asks you "How many people work in your company?" and you reply "About half," your Singaporean colleague will think that the employees are lazy and the company must surely go bankrupt. Even if you smile when saying this, remember that in Singapore this could be a sign that you are embarrassed by the lack of the work ethic in your company—not that you are not to be taken seriously.

The Chinese, Indians, and Malays do have a sense of humor, but it tends to be more of the slapstick variety.

CONCLUSION

E. M. Forster famously said that the first person you meet when you go abroad is yourself. Once outside the familiar boundaries of your own culture, your sense of self is challenged. This is partly what makes foreign travel so exciting. It is a learning experience that can be both interesting and demanding, and it can be a revelation to discover how you act and think in unfamiliar situations. If some of the many dos and don'ts listed here seem a little daunting—relax. The Singaporeans understand that you are a stranger in their land and will not expect you to be familiar with their customs, but they will be delighted if you attempt to learn something about their culture. This guide will set you on the road toward a fuller appreciation of this uniquely rich and varied society.

Further Reading

Braddon, Russell. *The Naked Island*. Edinburgh: Berlin, 2002.

Clavell, James. *King Rat*. U.S.A.: Dell, 1986.

Craig, JoAnn Meriwether. *Culture Shock! Singapore: A Guide to Customs and Etiquette*. Portland, Oregon: Graphic Arts Center Publishing, 1993/London: Kuperard, 2001.

Eliot, Joshua. *Footprint Singapore Handbook*. U.K.: Footprints Handbooks, 2001.

Keay, John. *The Honourable Company: A History of the English East India Company*. London: HarperCollins, 1991.

Lee Kuan Yew. *From Third World to First: The Singapore Story 1965–2000*. New York: HarperCollins, 2000.

Lewis, Mark. *The Rough Guide to Singapore*. New York: Rough Guides, 2003.

Nichol, John. *Singapore: The Bradt Travel Guide*. U.S.A.: Globe Pequot Press, 2002.

Seagrave, Sterling. *Lords of the Rim: The Invisible Empire of the Overseas Chinese*. U.S.A.: Putnam Publishing, 2000.

SarDesai, D.R. *Southeast Asia: Past & Present*. Colorado: Westview Press, 2003.

TalkingCock.com. *The Coxford Singlish Dictionary*. Singapore: Angsana Books, 2002.

Tan, Kok Seng. *Son of Singapore: Autobiography of a Coolie*. Singapore: Heinemann Asia, 1989.

Wibisono, Djoko. *The Food of Singapore: Authentic Recipes from the Manhattan of the East*. Singapore: Periplus Editions, 1995.

Wise, Michael. *Travellers' Tales of Old Singapore*. Connecticut: Weatherhill, 1996.

Index